Louis XIV and the Greatness of France

MAURICE ASHLEY

Louis XIV and the Greatness of France

THE FREE PRESS
A DIVISION OF MACMILLAN PUBLISHING CO., INC.
New York

This title first appeared as a volume in the Teach Yourself History series under the general editorship of A. L. Rowse.

First printed 1946

THE FREE PRESS
A DIVISION OF MACMILLAN PUBLISHING CO., INC.
866 Third Avenue, New York, N.Y. 10022

Printed in the United States of America

FIRST FREE PRESS PAPERBACK EDITION 1965

printing number

11 12 13 14 15 16 17 18 19 20

Contents

Chapter 1

The Rising Sun

KING LOUIS XIII, the second Bourbon King of France, and Anne of Austria, the sister of the Habsburg Philip IV of Spain, were the parents of Louis XIV, and they detested each other. The mother was a beautiful woman, tall with curly chestnut hair, a fair complexion, and magnificent white hands. She was a flirt, a gossipmonger, and rather lazy, but not without strength of character. Her husband was pious and melancholy, shy of women, devoted to his dogs and his mother. His mother set him against his wife, but he was forced to send his mother into exile because of her political intrigues. So he was not fated to enjoy life. He sought comfort in platonic friendships with the ladies of his wife's court. One young girl, Mlle de La Fayette, gave Louis XIII an occasional glimpse of happiness. She could laugh or be serious as the occasion demanded and the King was most at ease when he talked with her or heard her sing in the Queen's apartments. But one day Mlle de La Fayette decided it was better that she retired from Court into a convent. The King continued to visit her at the Sisters of St. Mary, and one day talked long with her through the grille. Finding it was too late to return to his palace at Saint-Germain that night, the King was obliged to go to the Louvre, where he shared the Queen's bed. And that night Louis XIV was conceived.

The birth of Louis XIV on September 5, 1638, was reckoned to be a miracle. His mother and father had been married for twenty-three years and this, their first child, seemed to be the product of a nation's prayers. It was no wonder that he was named Louis Dieu-donné—the God-given child. On her son Anne of Austria lavished all the love and care which her husband had refused. The un-

7

happy Louis XIII was not destined to see his son grow to
youth. After his baptism Louis Dieu-donné was presented to his father, who asked his name. "Louis XIV,"
was the reply. "Not yet, not yet," replied the dying King.
Before he died Louis XIII attempted to safeguard the
future of the kingdom by publishing a declaration establishing a Council of Regency which would have prevented
power from coming fully into the hands of the Queen
and of his cowardly and treacherous brother Gaston of
Orleans, both of whom he distrusted. The courtiers and
the lawyers all promised Louis XIII faithfully that they
would respect his last wishes. No sooner was the King
dead, however, than his instructions were overruled.
Wearing the violet of royal mourning, the child Louis
XIV was brought to the Parliament of Paris, where he
went through the ceremony known as a "Bed of Justice"
necessary to cancel his father's declaration. And thus his
mother, Anne of Austria, became regent without restraint.
When Louis XIV succeeded to the throne on May 14,
1643, the power of France and the absolute rights of the
monarchy had been fortified by the genius of Cardinal
Richelieu, the skilful and determined first Minister of
Louis XIII. The internal history of sixteenth-century
France had been dominated by the wars of religion between the Catholics and the Reformers, and it was not
until after many years of intrigue, civil war, and assassination that Henry IV, the first Bourbon ruler, a Protestant
turned Catholic, had imposed some measure of political
unity on the country. When he in turn was murdered civil
war soon broke out again, the Queen Mother Marie of
Medici, after her incompetent and pernicious regency was
over, joining with the rebels against her own son. Cardinal
Richelieu then set about solving the King's problems. He
obtained religious peace by confirming the toleration
granted to French Protestants by Henry IV, while preventing the dismemberment of the kingdom by defeating them
on the battlefield. Secondly, he repressed the anarchist
tendencies of the French nobility by governing the provinces largely through powerful agents, known as Intend-

ants, directly responsible to the throne. Finally, he sought to raise French prestige in Europe and to extend the national frontiers by engaging in the Thirty Years War against the Habsburg Holy Roman Emperor and the King of Spain in alliance with Protestant German princes and other Protestant Powers. Richelieu, ruthless, widely hated, and feared even by his master, died in December 1642. "Ah! if there is a God," it was said, "he will soon pay for what he has done; but if there is no God, then truly he is an able man." On his deathbed he was invited to forgive his enemies. "I have no enemies," was the stern reply, "but those of the State." He left an heir to his policy in another Cardinal, the Neapolitan Mazarin.

Mazarin, who was never a parish priest, first distinguished himself as an infantry officer in the papal army. A diplomatic career brought him to Paris, where in due course he was taken into the service of Richelieu; he was naturalized in 1639 and became a cardinal in 1641. He did not have the ruthlessness of his master, preferring to attain his ends by subtlety and flattery. Anne of Austria, convinced that he was utterly unlike Richelieu, whom she had loathed, took him as her chief adviser in preference to her first favourite. But the public was not deceived: "he is not dead—this cardinal, he has but changed his age." And indeed Mazarin pursued the foreign policy of Richelieu faithfully, varying his methods but maintaining the same objectives. Mazarin's position was strengthened by victories against Spain and the Emperor in the closing years of the Thirty Years War, while an unsuccessful attempt at his assassination by a disgruntled nobleman in 1643 induced the Queen to exile or imprison most of his rivals. But the richest source of strength was that the Queen Regent fell in love with him. According to one account, they were married, although this does not seem probable. At least they were bound together by the deepest bonds known to the human spirit. Mazarin's application, his tolerance, his statesmanship and, above all, his profound knowledge of foreign affairs fitted him to guide the monarchy during the tortuous years of Louis XIV's minority. He had many faults, particularly a possessiveness both for himself and for his family which degenerated into avarice in his old age, but his virtues were many. Above all, he was a magnificent paymaster for the French Army—"his principle was to go to the army as often as he could and always to carry money to it; taking care to provide the soldiers with all their little necessities." Among his many duties Mazarin was made responsible for the King's education. It is often said that he neglected it. This may be true in the technical sense—for Mazarin was no pedagogue—but it is certain that Louis learned many valuable political lessons from the Cardinal. "He was a minister," wrote Louis XIV in his *Memoirs,* "re-established in power against the wishes of many factions, very clever, very adroit, who loved me and whom I loved, who did me great services, even if his ideas and manners were naturally different from my own."

The young King was certainly spoiled and badly educated in the academic sense. His charming but vapid mother doted on him. He was given a marquis as his governor and an abbé as his tutor, but as a child he often fell into the hands of the junior ladies-in-waiting or was left to his own devices. He soon demonstrated that he had the enormous appetite of the Bourbon family and on one occasion was chased from the royal kitchen for his excesses. As he grew older he found his chief pleasures in listening to music and practising dance steps. When he was first called upon to attend meetings of the royal council he would frequently retire into the bathroom with a gentleman-in-waiting to play the guitar and discuss the ballet. "Games, dances, and comedies are the King's sole pursuits," recorded the Venetian ambassador in Paris with disapprobation in 1652.

Louis was given a free hand in his pleasures in part because his elders were harassed by most complicated problems of state. Civil wars forced the Court into exile and steady and continuous education became impossible. At Fontainebleau the King spent many hours bathing in the Seine with his governor or in strolling in the forest through which they had to pass in order to reach the river—"the dust of one being washed off by the other." His spirits were always high and he had his own way. One day he complained about the carriage which was to take him down to bathe and promptly ordered five new ones. One significant fact, however, is recorded by Mme de Motteville: "I often noticed with astonishment that in his games and amusements the King never laughed."

The King's curriculum consisted mainly of modern languages, dancing, drawing, and riding, although we are told that he translated Cæsar's commentaries; nevertheless he did not reach an advanced stage in Latin, which he afterwards found was a handicap. His education in the art of kingship was more complete. His valet de chambre sat in front of him with his hat on "to teach the King his profession." And each night he read aloud to his master from an appropriate history of France. The King promised "to follow the example of the most generous of his ancestors, particularly abhorring Louis the Idle." His tutor wrote a history of Henry IV for his especial benefit, and Catherine of Medici's letters of advice to her son, Henry III, were ceremoniously presented to him. The King recorded in later years the deep impression made upon him by his early history lessons: "From my childhood I loathed the mere mention of kings of straw and mayors of the palace." It was borne in upon him from a dozen sources that the duty of a king was not merely to reign but to rule and that kingship was a profession at once delightful and exacting. At an early age he practised absolutism by subjecting his young brother, Philip of Orleans, to his orders. He was constantly reminded of his powers. Even his writing master set him as an exercise the sentence: "Homage is due to kings. They do what they please."

So whatever the defects of his education, all his preceptors combined to fashion the complete monarch with charm of manner and a will of iron. There is, therefore, no basis for the story that Cardinal Mazarin used his power to prevent the enlightenment or instruction of his

King. On the contrary, that subtle Italian had chosen him as his own heir in the government of France. He protected him as if he were his own son. One day when King and Cardinal were dining with that elderly scoundrel Gaston of Orleans and lewd songs were begun, the Cardinal told the King to leave the table. Equally, although Mazarin was a prodigious gambler himself, he refused to allow the King money to dissipate at the gaming tables. As soon as the King was of age the Cardinal took him to meetings of the Council and explained to him the mysteries of politics. Louis XIV's education was directed to what were regarded as its proper ends and owed little to books.

Interspersed with the daily round of pleasures and lessons came those little ceremonies which are associated with monarchy. There was his father's funeral, where the monks of St. Denis quarrelled over pieces of gold, a visit of thanksgiving to Notre Dame after a bout of smallpox, ceremonies in the Parliament of Paris, the grand cavalcade of coming of age when he was thirteen. At the latter ceremony the King wore a coat "so covered with gold embroidery that neither the stuff nor its colour could be seen" and he rode a cream-coloured horse "the gay spirit of which exemplified the words of Plutarch that horses never flatter kings." By the time that he had reached adolescence Louis was considered a handsome young man "with a fine figure and a good countenance which made everyone admire him." He had a martial yet modest bearing, a sharp nose, thick sensual lips, and a fresh complexion unmarred yet by the smallpox. At first he seemed quiet and shy, but that was because he was anxious lest he should not be found "perfect in all things" as he "dreaded to be found to fail in anything." He was, in fact, cultivating that habit of reserve which, combined with courtesy and charm, are the professional armour of a man in authority. Throughout his youth under the influence of his picked teachers he had meditated to himself upon the high duties and privileges of his calling. He was determined to be a polished and godlike king. And he had already derived certain definite ideas from the political circumstances of his youth which had been distracted by the civil wars known as the Fronde.

The Fronde was a name bestowed upon the French civil wars of 1649–1653 after a game played by small boys who launched stones from a catapult and run away when the police arrived. This nickname reflects not unfairly the ultimate character of the conflict; but in the beginning the agitation which heralded the war was largely a genuine expression of national grievances not unlike that which preceded the English civil wars. As in England world economic causes had stopped the monarchy from being able to live on the income from its own estates and upon its traditional sources of revenue. The series of foreign wars on which the French had engaged had raised taxation to unparalleled heights. These taxes were irritating and inequitable, especially as many privileged classes were exempted from them. Their collection fell into the hands of financiers on the make who were not nice or tactful about their methods of administration. Moreover, the French rentiers had an additional grievance in that their funds were no longer properly secured. The French Parliament, a gathering of lawyers with the right to register royal edicts and to make "humble remonstrances," was the only body available to express their widespread grievances. It took the opportunity afforded by Louis XIV's minority to do so with vigour. "It is ten years," said one speaker in 1648, "since the country was ruined: the peasants are reduced to sleeping on straw: their furniture is sold for the payment of taxes, and to supply Paris with luxuries millions of innocent souls are obliged to live on black and oaten bread." In the summer of 1648 this body boldly put forward a list of remedies, among others that no taxes should be levied except in virtue of edicts or declarations duly verified by the law courts, and that no French subject should be kept in prison for more than twenty-four hours without being brought to justice. The Regency capitulated to Parliament's demands except for the article on personal freedom, but did so with obvious reluctance.

The Queen's disgust was communicated to the child King. After the French army had won a great victory over the Spaniards at Lens in August 1649—a victory about which the King was heard to say "it would disappoint those people in Parliament"—the Queen struck. Broussel, an old and distinguished Parliamentary councillor, popular, incorruptible, and disinterested, was placed under arrest. His cry had been "Fewer taxes—no taxes." The news of his arrest electrified Paris and led to immediate revolt. "The mob has taken up arms," complained the Queen, "the barricades have been put up in the streets . . . this is only the beginning; the evil may grow to a point where the royal authority will be destroyed." With unruly Parisians, discontented bourgeoisie, and an inept ruler, it was the veritable presage of the French Revolution. But from then on the strength of the opposition to the Crown declined. There was no Mirabeau or Robespierre to harness the forces that had been unloosed; Parliament was a closed body too clearly interested for the most part in its own privileges. The rebel movement was fostered and perverted by those elements among an irresponsible nobility which had delighted to fish in troubled waters in earlier reigns. Descendants of royal bastards, lovely ladies, who preferred "the honourable crime of lèse-majesté" to living with their husbands, the whole crew manipulated and directed by the sinister ecclesiastic De Retz, plunged eagerly into the battle. When the leaders in Parliament found that these nobles were conspiring with foreign enemies they agreed to treat with the Crown, and after limited fighting around Paris the first civil war came to an end.

There followed an uneasy truce before a second civil war began. The disgruntled nobles, seeing the chances offered by the weakness of the Queen and the unpopularity of Cardinal Mazarin, prepared to play their old games again. The Parisians were stirred up and frightened by the idea that the Court might leave the capital, as it had done during the first Fronde. One day in 1651 a crowd of Parisians forced their way into the Palais Royal and demanded to see the King. The Queen gave orders that they were to be admitted. They stared at the King as he lay asleep for a long time and "whereas they had entered the palace like furies, they left it full of gentleness, asking God with all their hearts to protect their young King, whose presence had the power to charm them." It was said (and it is likely enough) that the King was not really asleep; and that this incident made a permanent and unhappy impression upon his mind.

During the second Fronde Cardinal Mazarin twice went into voluntary exile; two of the most successful French generals of the Thirty Years War fought against each other; and conditions in Paris and in some part of the provinces became anarchic. Orleans was closed to the King's army by the amazon princess, "Mademoiselle," the King's own cousin. Republican ideas were mooted in rebel Bordeaux. But the monarchy profited from dissensions among its enemies, and the incurable frivolity of the leaders of the Fronde betrayed them. In October 1652 the King returned in triumph to Paris and recalled Mazarin. The Cardinal, of whom it has been said that "never did a man with so much power and so many enemies pardon so easily and imprison so few," was lenient. The King, now a boy of fifteen, was less so. De Retz, the chief of the Frondeurs, who had got himself created cardinal, finally ventured to come to Court. "The King," related Mme de Motteville, "employing on this occasion that judicious moderation which has since been so admirably practised by him in all his actions, looked pleasantly at the Cardinal and asked him if he had seen the Queen. De Retz having answered no, he invited him amiably to follow him. And at the same time he ordered Villequier, captain of his guards, to arrest him the moment he should leave the Queen, which was done punctually. Thus ended in him the last of the Fronde."

The King obtained several lessons from the Fronde which he never forgot and which shaped his policy as a ruler. He learned to suspect the nobility and refused to entrust them with responsible positions in the State. They were allowed to retain their privileges, but Louis confirmed Richelieu's policy of depriving them of their administrative duties. Equally the King hated and feared the "canaille" and, above all, the people of Paris who had dared to peer into his bedchamber. Hence he was to remove his Court to Versailles out of reach of the rebellious capital. Finally, he saw the dangers of an unpopular first Minister who had to be protected by the divinity that doth hedge a king. He had seen shining far too brightly that "malignant star which threatened the welfare of kings." So far as in him lay, it should not shine again in his lifetime.

After the Court had returned to Paris and as the King neared the end of his teens, he began to worship both Venus and Mars. To hasten the close of the long-drawn-out war against Spain, Cardinal Mazarin had not hesitated to ally himself with the heretical regicide, Oliver Cromwell. Louis visited Mardyke in Flanders, which was besieged by Anglo-French forces. His first sight of war was not pleasant. The place was infected with rotten corpses and the French soldiers were without sufficient food or pay. The King fell ill at Calais and soon returned to Fontainebleau. In the affairs of the heart he was also unfortunate. Mazarin had five attractive nieces named Mancini whom he brought to the Court to become the playmates of the King. The girls tempered a passionate Italian temperament (their father was a Roman nobleman) with an eye to the main chance. The King was first attracted by the second niece, Olympe Mancini, a beautiful and charming woman, while at the little balls which enlivened the life of the Court he honoured the eldest Mancini sister, the Duchesse de Mercoeur, by dancing with her in preference even to Princess Henrietta of England. But early in 1657 Mme de Mercoeur died, Olympe married, and Louis turned his attention to the "ugly duckling" of the Mancini family, the middle sister, Marie, thus keeping his affections upon an approved and reliable pattern.

The story of Louis XIV and Marie Mancini has usually

been told in somewhat disparaging terms by historians, probably because the records are derived from sour women who had never known love themselves, in particular from the *Memoirs* of Mme de Motteville who thankfully relinquished the married state after two years with an octogenarian. Marie, if we may judge from her portraits, was a pretty girl and she was certainly attractive, ambitious, and well-read. She afforded a pleasing contrast with her stately but stupid sister, Olympe, and with an agreeable young girl, Mlle de la Motte, on whom the King had cast his eyes but who soon disappeared into a convent. Marie Mancini had emerged with some difficulty from one. She was bold and fiery, with a power to provoke which proved irresistible to this shy mother's darling. She became Louis's constant companion; they talked together, read romantic novels, and grew inseparable. The snobs and old maids of the Court would not admit, however, that they were in love. The Cardinal and the Queen Mother strongly disapproved of the affair as soon as they recognized its seriousness. For at this date they were planning the King's marriage and Anne of Austria, herself a Spanish princess, had set her heart on the King's wedding her niece, the Spanish Infanta, daughter of King Philip IV, and on thus bringing to an end the interminable French war against her native land.

Mazarin also favoured the match for diplomatic reasons, although he first held out hopes to Princess Marguerite of Savoy as an inducement to the King of Spain to make an urgent offer. The family party set out in 1658 to meet Princess Marguerite at Lyons; but the King took Marie Mancini with him. The marriage negotiations fell through (as was intended) and for a while the King's love for Marie deepened. When his mother remonstrated with him he lost his temper. The Cardinal took an equally stern line with his niece. Marie was provocative: "Are you not ashamed," she asked Louis, "that they want to give you such an ugly wife?" According to one account, he went on his knees to the Queen and the Cardinal and begged their permission for him to marry his beloved.

Marie unquestionably had hopes. But both were made to see where their duty lay. There were tears and protestations, but they obeyed the necessities of State. The King went to the Pyrenees to meet the Infanta and in order not to compromise national prestige the bride and bridegroom had their first conversation sitting upon seats which were carefully placed upon the frontier line between France and Spain. Maria Theresa was a pretty little thing, innocent, ignorant, and anxious to be loved. They were married by double proxy in June 1660.

Marie Mancini married an Italian nobleman, Count Colonna, and departed for Italy. When she left, the King saw her to her carriage. As Marie entered her carriage, Louis "uttered a sigh, but did not say a word; then he bowed deeply over the carriage door in honour of the princess, who burst into tears, and the carriage drove away." Colonna was surprised to find that his wife was a virgin.

The Queen Mother was concerned—rightly, as events proved—over the success of the King's marriage of convenience. She knew her son "to be rather cold and grave," wrote Mme de Motteville, "and owned to us that she had felt grave misgivings lest the indifference which she imagined to be in the King's soul should prove injurious to this niece whom she so ardently desired to make him marry." A moving and dramatic scene had taken place between Louis XIV and his mother before he had finally renounced Marie Mancini. "I pity the King," said Anne of Austria after that interview, "he is both loving and reasonable and God gave him the loftiness necessary to be a great king." Certainly from that time forward Louis made a clear distinction in his mind between his "duties" and his "pleasures." And there is little doubt that his youthful experience had a searing effect on his whole life.

Soon after the King's marriage and the signature of the Peace of the Pyrenees, which brought the Spanish war to an end, Mazarin's health declined. In his last years his rule had been almost despotic; he was as powerful, it was said, "as God the Father at the beginning of the world." Even the Queen Mother, who remained passionately devoted to him, complained that he was growing ill-humoured and miserly. When he had been exiled during the Fronde he lost all his possessions, and on his restoration to power he rebuilt his fortune swiftly and without scruple. But Louis XIV trusted his Minister to the end. The relations between them never ceased to be intimate. When after his visit to the front in 1658 Louis had imagined that he was dying he told the Cardinal that he was the best friend he had. One contemporary writer considered indeed that there was an "occult sympathy" between the King and the Cardinal. It is possible that Louis knew that the Italian was in effect, if not in name, his stepfather. And the Cardinal in return taught his master all that he could be taught of his knowledge of statecraft, including the advantages of dissimulation.

Now, however, Mazarin knew that it was time to put his affairs in order and to dispose of his fortune. He took a reluctant last look at his worldly treasures. "See, my friend," he told an intimate as they stood in his galleries, "that beautiful picture of Correggio and that Venus of Titian, and that incomparable Deluge of Annibale Carracci, for I know you love pictures and understand them; ah! my poor friend, must I quit all that? Adieu, dear pictures, I have loved so well and which cost so much!" Such were his last regrets; he showed no fear of death; "courage!" he exclaimed, "to suffer is necessary." He died in March 1661.

The Court was astonished when it learned that the King had decided to become his own Prime Minister. But Louis had long made up his mind to do so, and that had been Mazarin's own advice to him. He announced publicly that he did not approve of the life of a do-nothing king and ordered Le Tellier, de Lionne, and Fouquet, the three able ministers bequeathed to him by Mazarin, to make their reports in future to him personally. Convinced that the profession of a king was "splendid, noble, and delightful," he was fully prepared to undertake all the labours that were necessary for its exercise. He put away childish things and devoted his modest abilities to the government of his country; its glories, its adventures, its conquests should in future be his and no other's.

Chapter 2

The King and His Kingdom

LOUIS XIV was twenty-two-and-a-half years old when Mazarin died and he began personally to rule his kingdom. Though not tall, he was every inch a king. Universally considered handsome, Louis was at once charming, serious, polite, calm, and irresistibly gracious. Mme de Motteville described him as he appeared to her in 1661:

> He was agreeable personally, civil, and easy of approach to all; but with a lofty and serious air which impressed everyone with respect and awe and prevented even his confidential advisers from forgetting his position when they engaged in private conversation with him—although he was gay and familiar with the ladies.

His sense of dignity and pride in his divine office were profound and he was on more than nodding terms with the Deity. As God (he considered) was "infinitely jealous of His glory" so too must the French King be. Whether or not he actually said "I am the State" is disputed, but he certainly believed it. He identified himself with the glory rather than the well-being of his subjects, whom he did not trust. What he regarded as the treachery of the nobility towards his ancestors in previous reigns and towards himself during the wars of the Fronde was never forgotten. He employed as his chief ministers middle-class administrators who might be relied upon to be loyal. But he confessed in his *Memoirs* that he was equally suspicious of those who had openly rebelled against him and those who paraded their dutifulness. "There is scarcely any loyalty," he said cynically, "which cannot be bought with money or high honours." Hence in dealing with individuals he invariably practised the arts of dissimulation which he had learnt from Mazarin and perhaps from the example of his Medici ancestors.

At this stage of his life the King was by no means a

religious enthusiast. He was devoted to no one but his mother, who was to die in torments. Although he kept himself fit by daily hunting and other forms of exercise, he paid for his love of food with lifelong dyspepsia. He found his relaxation with the Court beauties. Soon after his marriage he took a mistress, in spite of his mother's remonstrances, and continued to indulge his passions until he reached a respectable old age spent in the company of the religious Mme de Maintenon. He was attracted by Mlle de la Motte-Houdancourt, whom he met in the rooms of his old flame, Olympe Mancini, now Countess de Soissons. He often used to talk with this young lady in the apartment of the Maids of Honour through a hole in the pine board partition. When the Duchess de Navailles, who was in charge of the Maids of Honour, ventured to protest at this habit of the King, he procured her dismissal. Mlle de la Motte-Houdancourt hesitated to meet the King's wishes in order to raise her value, but was unable to oust her rival, the blonde and blue-eyed Louise de la Vallière, who was genuinely devoted to the King and had readily yielded to "those delicate passions which in ordinary people are called vices."

But these indulgences did not prevent the King from taking his profession with the utmost seriousness. "If you let yourself be carried away by your passions," he said, "don't do it in business hours." Glory, he considered, was worth effort and care. In a famous passage in his *Memoirs* he wrote:

> Love of glory requires the same delicacy of touch and of approach as love of a woman. Although I was enthusiastic to make a name for myself, I was fearful of failure and, since committing the slightest fault filled me with a deep sense of shame, I decided to take the greatest possible care in my behaviour.

As he began to master the art of kingship he felt himself spiritually uplifted and enjoyed his labours. His early timidity in handling people and affairs of State soon disappeared—"it seemed to me that I was a king and born to be one." Nevertheless it was noticed that all through his reign he spoke slowly and with deliberation, determined to avoid the least mistake which might detract from his dignity. Prudence was always his watchword and he never really imagined that to rule was as easy as it was pleasant.

From the very beginning Louis worked long hours and planned his days methodically. "Give me an almanac and a watch," wrote the Duke of Saint-Simon, "and even if I am three hundred leagues away from him I will tell you what the King is doing." He worked from six to nine hours a day. Although he usually went to bed very late, he got up at eight or nine and worked every morning from ten to twelve-thirty. Then he attended Mass, dined and spent some time with his family. Later in the afternoon he usually went back to work with his ministers and gave audiences. At busy times he would hold three council meetings a day, the last one not ending until ten o'clock at night. In the early years of his reign he often shut himself up for two hours to study Latin, since he was determined to be able to read the diplomatic documents written in that language. In brief the King was a model of diligence and spared neither himself nor his ministers. If hard work alone could have produced a great statesman, he would have been one.

What were the main problems which Louis XIV had to solve? The labours of his grandfather, Henry IV, of Richelieu and of Mazarin had made this nation of some eighteen million inhabitants without question the leading State in seventeenth century Europe. The old Europe reached its closing stages when the renegade German monk Martin Luther had in 1517 nailed his ninety-five theses to the door of Wittenberg church and the Emperor Charles V had in 1556 divided his European domain, which was comparable in size with that of Charlemagne, into two parts and retired to indulge his large appetite at a monastery in Estremadura. The two Habsburg rulers who shared the Emperor Charles V's inheritance were unable to maintain their power intact. The Habsburg "Holy Roman" Emperors who ruled from Vienna over Austria, Bohemia, and Hungary found their authority disputed by the rise of Lutheran and later Calvinist Protestantism. Spain was defeated in turn by England, the United Netherlands, and by Portugal.

When the two Habsburg rulers were involved in the Thirty Years War in Germany, Cardinal Richelieu perceived the opportunity to enhance the power and extend the territories of the French kingdom. "I wished," he said, "to restore to Gaul the limit which nature designed for her . . . to identify Gaul with France," that is, he wished to win for France the "natural boundaries" of the Alps, the Pyrenees, and the Rhine. To this end he built up a large army and navy and subsidized Protestant princes to fight the Habsburgs. France was at war for twenty-five years to fulfil this policy of expansion in search of security. Mazarin brought Richelieu's policy to a successful conclusion. By the treaty of Westphalia (1648) the French monarchy acquired the Emperor's rights over Alsace (excluding Strasbourg), and the three bishoprics of Metz, Toul, and Verdun, lying west of Lorraine, were annexed to the French Crown. By the Treaty of the Pyrenees (1659), which closed the long war between France and Spain, the provinces of Artois, Roussillon, and Cerdagne were absorbed into France, although Lorraine—except for Thionville—was given up. This treaty was cemented by Louis XIV's marriage to the Spanish Infanta. By an ambiguously worded clause in the marriage treaty Maria Theresa's renunciation of her possible claim to the Spanish throne was apparently made (according to French interpretation) to depend upon the payment of a large dowry by her father. The dowry was never paid. Louis XIV himself was of course of Habsburg descent (through his mother), and both he and his wife were of the direct line of the Emperor Charles V. This was to prove a decisive factor in Louis's foreign policy.

The defeat of the Habsburgs in the middle of the seventeenth century made France supreme in Europe. Germany was divided and exhausted, her people having acquired that slavish resignation to perpetual war which became one of their least pleasing characteristics. Leopold I, who was elected Habsburg Emperor in 1658 at the age of seventeen, was only the nominal overlord of the loose confederation of German States. In Vienna, the Imperial capital, life was placid. In Austria, it was said, "it was always Sunday." The rulers of Spain, where the climate and the influence of colonial wealth made for laziness, proved incapable of sustaining the burden of world-wide empire. Maria Theresa's stepbrother, who was to become King Charles II of Spain, was born a weakling and grew up an invalid, and the Spanish line seemed faced with extinction. The Protestant Powers, England, the United Provinces (Holland), and Sweden (including Finland and Estonia), were in 1661 all allies of France, and although they had each enjoyed military successes under able leaders (Cromwell, William the Silent, Gustavus Adolphus) their populations and resources appeared too small to rival the magnificence of France—unless of course they were united against her. Poland's history "alternated between vast conquests and mortal peril." The Turks still threatened Eastern Europe but were a declining Power. Italy was then but a geographical expression; and who was to suspect that the clever "Great Elector" of Brandenburg, who ruled East Prussia and East Pomerania also, was to fashion a State which was to bring suffering to France three times in later centuries?

France was therefore the dominant power in Europe. Louis XIV had inherited a kingdom enlarged on the frontiers, with the most powerful army, the most skilful generals, and the best-trained diplomatic service in Europe. He had before him the choice of either extending the frontiers of his country (which remained militarily precarious at least to the north-east) and pushing to an annihilating victory the dynastic struggle of Bourbon and Habsburg, or of consolidating his gains and increasing them by cautious diplomatic action. In view of his opportunities and his upbringing there could be little doubt that he would incline to the bolder and more aggressive policy.

But, judged by the most realistic and calculating standards of statesmanship the immediate choice was less easy than appeared. For France had paid a heavy price for her victories and the nation needed time to recuperate.

The internal history of France during the first half of the seventeenth century was indeed largely a story of the mounting burdens of public finance. The French King, like the King of England, was unable to "live of his own" and the expedients to which the Treasury was driven to raise money caused widespread misery and positive discontent. The systems of taxation which prevailed were, moreover, wildly inequitable. The principal tax, the "taille," was not levied on the clergy, nobility, public and local officials of all types, or on free towns. In some areas it fell on personal as well as on real property. No minister, not even Henry IV's skilful Minister Sully, renowned for his financial probity, had felt strong enough to do more than tinker with its worst abuses. The collectors were often cruel or corrupt; nevertheless they frequently received more abuse than money and had to make up out of their own pockets the difference between the amount of the assessment and the yield. In 1646 three thousand persons had been imprisoned for failing to pay the taille. In 1655 a report was sent to England that the French people were so overwhelmed with "misery, tailles, and all sorts of taxes" that they were little better off than in wartime. The "gabelle" or salt tax was equally unfair and varied enormously in its incidence between different parts of the country. Salt was a necessity for preserving food, but in some places poor people were obliged to buy a fixed amount of salt (which was a Government monopoly) whether they needed it or not. Indirect taxes included heavy export and import duties and local customs. Except under the careful and able management of Sully direct and indirect taxation failed to raise sufficient revenue to balance the budget. Other expedients commonly used to raise money for the Crown were the sale of offices, the alienation of the royal domain, and the debasement of the coinage. The methods by which taxes were collected were wasteful. The farmers and commissioners of taxes made large sums at the national expense; in one year only two-thirds of the yield of the taille reached the Treasury.

There was also no adequate control over the central administration of public finance. The powers of the controller (superintendant) of finance were virtually unlimited, provided he had the confidence of the king. Particelli d'Emery, who had been appointed to this office by Mazarin, had to be dismissed owing to the fury of the Frondeurs and of Parliament. His office was divided between two successors, one of whom, Nicholas Fouquet, a brilliant and ambitious man, was ultimately imprisoned for embezzlement and other crimes.

The long wars waged by Richelieu and Mazarin caused the financial position, temporarily set right by Sully, to deteriorate. The regency of Anne of Austria was a terrible period for French finance. Anne was said to be willing to giving anything to anybody and could never refuse a favour. Mazarin preferred to buy off his enemies rather than to fight them. The principal cause of the first Fronde had been grievances over taxation and the extravagances of Cardinal Mazarin.

To meet the gap between public revenue and expenditure resort was made to borrowing. Financiers known as "traitants" were employed to raise large sums of money on the security of future taxes or of the royal estates. France has always been a country where people save readily and regularly and a class of lenders was soon forthcoming to invest in the funds. These "rentiers," as they were called, were given a generous rate of interest, but were always eager to protest when they considered that they were ill-treated by conversions or by actions jeopardizing the funds upon which their loans were secured. By an elaborate system of borrowing the State was able to pledge its future income, and the royal revenues during the minority of Louis XIV were usually consumed three years in advance. In 1661 it was estimated that the royal revenue amounted to some 31,000,000 livres, of which 9,000,000 had to be spent on interest payments, while there was a floating debt of over 60,000,000 livres.

These financial difficulties might have been surmounted

if the country had been economically prosperous, but the kingdom over which Louis XIV now began to rule had been suffering from a depression which had hit the whole of western Europe in the late sixteen-fifties. The universal opinion in France at the end of the Spanish war was that the country was ruined. A series of bad harvests, epidemics, and floods had swept the country. Industry had fallen into decay; the peasants were burdened by the complicated and incompetently administered system of taxation; much French commerce had been filched by the enterprising Dutch and English.

Yet the land over which Louis XIV ruled ought to have been prosperous. The soil of the country was naturally rich and varied, the people industrious and thrifty, the weather normally kindly. "To establish the grandeur of the French monarchy," wrote an Italian observer in 1661, "Heaven itself has given the nation almost miraculous gifts. It is full of fertile land . . . excellently situated upon two oceans, watered by many navigable rivers which flow in all directions . . . well populated . . . rich in wealth and in soldiers." The foundation of the national economy was agriculture. In 1661 the real cultivators, the peasantry, owned only about one-fifth of the soil. Not only were they burdened by heavy taxation, rents and customary dues, but restrictions upon export and even upon the transport of their produce from province to province were imposed in the interests of a mistaken economic system. Consequently farmers seldom obtained the best price for their wheat and at times there was starvation in the midst of plenty. Richelieu's policy had injured agriculture and the position had been worsened by the civil wars. Both agriculture and industry were damaged by the poor condition of internal communications; in 1661 the roads of France were in a shocking state. There may have been undue pessimism in the contemporary accounts of the condition of agriculture, but there could be no question about the decay of industry at this date. Most of the large-scale industries created with so much effort under Henry IV had completely vanished. The brass workers had disappeared, wool was no longer woven in Languedoc, the

silk manufacturers of Lyons and Tours were much reduced in size, and many iron-works and tanneries had
been completely abandoned. There was a great deal of
unemployment. Foreign trade was in little better condition.
Although France exported wines, silks, and articles of
furniture, and re-exported sugar, almost the whole of her
carrying trade was in the hands of foreigners who took a
substantial share of the profits. It was stated, perhaps with
some pessimism, that of the twenty thousand merchant
ships which sailed the seven seas only six hundred were
French; and for this reason the French people did not
derive much advantage from their widespread colonies in
Canada, West Africa, and the West Indies.

A severe and ill-considered tariff policy discouraged
foreign trade, just as the chaotic fiscal policy injured
domestic industry and agriculture. There were of course
loopholes in the laws. For example, as in England, there
were constant prohibitions upon luxury trades. These prohibitions were ignored by the privileged classes, who
bought glassware, carpets, and lace from abroad and
dressed and housed themselves in a way that made the
French Court the marvel of Europe.

Between the struggling peasantry and the craftsmen
earning a precarious livelihood in the towns, on the one
hand, and the privileged nobility and ecclesiastics, on the
other, a new class had now arisen in France, the bourgeoisie. As M. Seignobos has pointed out, the conception
of a comprehensive intermediate class known as the bourgeoisie was originally French. The term was applied both
to the professional classes and to those who lived upon
an independent income, generally men who had made a
fortune in trade and had perhaps purchased a patent
of nobility. A peculiar characteristic of the bourgeois was
that he regulated his expenditure according to his income,
whereas the nobility determined their expenditure by the
requirements of their rank and position, making up the
deficit by borrowing. The bourgeoise now began to play
a leading part in the State. Whereas in seventeenth-century
England the sense of social and political responsibility
among the aristocracy went deep, in France the nobility

proved itself to be largely frivolous and irresponsible, as was shown by its conduct in the wars of the Fronde. The result was that in France the monarchy came more and more to rely upon the bourgeoisie (even though it might be transformed into a new aristocracy) for the administration of public affairs. Though France might laugh with Molière at the "bourgeois gentleman" she found him serviceable. Louis XIV was therefore only to accentuate an almost unavoidable trend. At his Court the privileged aristocracy worshipped at the shrine of the Sun King and wrote readable memoirs recounting their worthless lives. But in the Councils of State it was the bourgeoisie who were labouring to magnify the royal glory. In the provinces the lower classes, in the face of every conceivable handicap, gradually improved their lot—and this improvement was in the end to make them all the more conscious and resentful of the injustices of the social system.

Such was the country over which Louis XIV was now to rule. Two obvious choices (as has been said) lay before him. He might, like his grandfather, Henry IV, have recognized the state of decay into which a potentially rich and prosperous nation had fallen through prolonged wars at home and abroad and have decided that his first duty was to allow it to recuperate before embarking on foreign adventures. Believing, as he declared in his *Memoirs,* that the monarchy required the support of every class and owed a duty to every class, Louis might have appreciated the difficulties under which the peasants and artisans laboured and have instituted a thoroughgoing reform of fiscal and administrative methods. On the other hand, he might have taken the opportunity presented to him by the successful foreign policy of Richelieu and Mazarin to complete their work, profiting from the strength of his armies and the weakness of his enemies. It is even possible that a ruler with sound military advice would have recognized the danger to France of the exposed and unprotected north-eastern frontiers, where the rivers offered routes and not barriers to the invader, and concentrated all his efforts upon rectifying this frontier, subsequently devoting himself to the consolidation of his gains.

But in fact Louis took neither the one choice nor the other. He acquiesced in certain attempts at fiscal reform but at the same time indulged in an aggressive foreign policy which was bound sooner or later to lead to war. He refused to follow his grandfather's policy of husbanding the national finances and thereby stimulating national prosperity. On the contrary, he soon displayed all the extravagances of his mother. There is no reason to suppose that he had at that date any real understanding of the sufferings of the peasantry who formed the hard core of his kingdom or that he had learnt any valuable lessons from his wanderings in the provinces during his minority. At the same time he did not engage upon a constructive foreign policy. Whatever the ultimate result of his aggressive foreign policy may have been, there is no evidence to show, as Professor Picavet has pointed out, that it was his intention to follow Richelieu's plan to extend French possessions until they reached the natural strategic frontiers. Both abroad and at home his policy was essentially to assert the authority and glory of kingship, and its object was prestige rather than security. He was conscientious but not enlightened in the exercise of his duties. And lacking a clear perception of policy he made serious mistakes. True, if genius could be limited to the simple formula of an infinite capacity for taking pains, Louis XIV would have been a great statesman, for he was assiduous in the extreme. But statesmanship requires more than that. And the reason why the reign of Louis XIV was to be a mighty age in French history—in spite of all that was to be said by a succession of the King's critics—was because the people over whom he ruled were outstanding in their industry, their intelligence, their wit, their courage, their patriotism, their catholicity of taste, and their artistic qualities. The courtier who lived in the harmony of his own little world, ignoring all that lay outside it, might assert that the glory of France in the mid-seventeenth century derived from her King. But the truth was that he was fortunate in being born to reign at a propitious moment over so fruitful a land and so talented a people.

Chapter 3

A Fine Italian Hand

IN THE "MEMOIRS" which he wrote in 1661 to advise his son about the problems of government Louis XIV coupled love of work with the pleasure of ruling. Although, he said, affairs of State might seem at first like those difficult and obscure passages in literature of which one easily grows bored, one soon realizes that the science of kingship consists mainly in the exercise of common sense, which is simple and even pleasant. Though the exercise of common sense is scarcely a fair way of describing Louis's method of government, it is certainly true that the King displayed surprising devotion to his labours. When he first ordered his ministers to report directly to him, the courtiers were sceptical and spoke of an ardour that would quickly cool, but he disappointed his critics. From the beginning his rule was purely personal and the machinery of government took the form of councils over many of which the King himself presided.

The most important of the councils was the Council of State of which the King's ministers alone were members. This council dealt with matters of diplomacy or war. It met in the royal apartments after dinner four times a week. Two other councils (Depêches and Finances) were concerned with internal affairs. A fourth council was a kind of privy council which heard appeals. Although this last council was normally presided over by the Chancellor, the King advised his son to attend it occasionally, if he had nothing more pressing to do, since the royal presence was inspiring to the councillors and he could thus learn what was going on in the kingdom.

The principal ministers at the outset of the King's period of personal rule were the Chancellor, the Superintendant of Finance (who corresponded roughly with the English Treasurer), and four Secretaries of State who divided the responsibility both for different provinces and different subjects. The Chancellor Séguier was a servile old man with a seamy past who wisely effaced himself. The Superintendant of Finance, Nicholas Fouquet, on the other hand, was a remarkable personality. Born in 1615, the thirteenth child of the Vicomte de Vaux, he had enjoyed a rapid rise to power. After attaining his high office at the age of thirty-seven, he had proved a bold and valuable servant of Mazarin. His versatility and charm were far-reaching. Not only was his knowledge of law and diplomacy solid, but he was a brilliant conversationalist and a discerning patron of the arts. Anne of Austria said of him that he would have been an unblemished genius had it not been for his love of beautiful women and buildings. Unfortunately for himself he was insufficiently interested in the details of the national finances for which he was responsible and he had a gift for making enemies as well as friends. Nevertheless, in 1661 he still seemed well in the saddle; he explained to the King that any financial peccadilloes that he might have committed were by Mazarin's order and were due to the exceptional circumstances of the times. The King appeared to understand and entrusted him with various confidential missions and diplomatic negotiations.

The Secretary of State for War was Michel Le Tellier, who had proved himself a successful army administrator in the closing years of the Thirty Years War and had been outstandingly loyal to the Queen Mother and to Mazarin during the Fronde. In 1661, however, he was beginning to hand over his duties to his son, the Marquis de Louvois, who was teachable, hard-working, and obedient. Another leading minister was Hugues de Lionne, who was the nephew of Servien, Fouquet's former partner in financial administration. Lionne specialized in foreign affairs and had a rich experience of diplomacy. He helped to negotiate both the Treaty of Westphalia and the Peace of the Pyrenees. Witty and accomplished, he enjoyed both work and play. He was to prove one of Louis XIV's most reliable servants.

All these statesmen had been recommended to the King by Mazarin; they were of modest parentage, exceptional abilities, and well able to feather their own nests. Another servant to whom the Cardinal had commended the King's patronage was his own personal factotum, the conscientious but unattractive Jean-Baptiste Colbert. Colbert, who was born in 1619 the son of a draper at Rheims, had been brought to the notice of Mazarin by Le Tellier and soon became the confidential adviser and trusted agent of the Chief Minister. He was unwearying in his devotion to the petty detail of the Cardinal's personal fortunes. He ostentatiously showed that he knew his place. Wearing sombre clothes and an austere look, he acquired the nickname of the "North" after that chilly wind, and announced that he "took no holiday, had no pleasure nor amusement and spent my whole life on the Cardinal's business—as what I love is work." He was obviously a man after the King's own heart and in due course became a member of all his councils. Nevertheless it must not be imagined that Colbert was any more disinterested in his own prospects or had a smaller inclination to nepotism than any of his fellow ministers.

Colbert at once drew the King's attention to the unsatisfactory condition of the national finances under the administration of Fouquet. Whether because he felt the way which the wind was blowing or not, Fouquet made a fatal mistake: he approached the King's mistress, La Vallière, and offered her money. The King determined on his ruin and set about it with the same kind of courtly deceit which he had employed against Cardinal de Retz nine years earlier. Fouquet held the post of Procureur-Général to the Parliament of Paris, which carried with it the right to be tried only by his parliamentary colleagues. Louis persuaded Fouquet to sell this office on the ground that it was incompatible with complete devotion to the interests of the Crown. It was said that the King feared that Fouquet had so many friends in Parliament and even abroad that a direct attack upon him might have started a new Fronde. Next Louis invited himself to an entertainment at Fouquet's palatial residence at Vaux, half-way between Fontainebleau and Paris. Delighted, Fouquet spared no effort to honour and amuse his master. Vaux was a beautiful estate filled with terraces, fountains, and cascades. It was said that the owner had divided a river into a thousand fountains and turned the contents of a thousand fountains into torrents. In his library there were 2,700 volumes, and his table service was made of gold. To this extraordinary fête, which cost tens of thousands of pounds, six thousand guests were invited; music was provided by Lully, the famous contemporary of Purcell, and a play by Molière. The King was indeed given every reason to wonder whether his Minister of Finance had plundered the Exchequer and whether so rich and powerful a subject did not cast a shadow upon the throne. Two months after the fête Fouquet was arrested for treason, the office of Superintendant of Finance abolished, and a Chamber of Justice created to try him and other suspected peculators.

The trial of Nicholas Fouquet lasted nearly three years. Colbert seized and tampered with his papers and built up the case against him without scruple. The parliamentary commissioners who acted as judges and jury included originally several men who were Fouquet's personal enemies or rivals. The first president was dismissed for his impartiality in the conduct of the trial. Finally the rights of the accused in preparing his defence were severely restricted, an attempt even being made to deprive him of the services of counsel. Nevertheless Fouquet defended himself with courage and dignity. His friends did not desert the fallen Minister in spite of the well known implacable enmity of the young King. The poet La Fontaine composed an ode in favour of clemency towards him, which Fouquet in prison submitted to a critical and impersonal analysis. His supporters even succeeded in smuggling a written defence out of prison and secretly printing and distributing it. Public opinion was not unsympathetic to the accused man, who claimed that the King had already fully forgiven him any sharp practices which he had carried out on Marzarin's behalf, while since the death of the Cardinal he had been responsible for no financial transactions which had not been countersigned by the King himself. He maintained that his own fortune had been created by legitimate means and that he had impoverished himself by staking his credit on the King's behalf. The prosecution failed to prove that Fouquet was guilty of treason but appeared to establish that his methods of financial administration were, to say the least, careless. The Chamber of Justice finally sentenced him to banishment. The King, who had hoped that Fouquet would be condemned to death, however, overruled the findings of the Court and ordered that the former Minister should be imprisoned for life. Fouquet, who had previously been lodged in various prisons, was taken from the Bastille to the fortress of Pignerol in Southern France on the Italian frontier.

Legend and fiction have grown up around the story of Fouquet, some saying that he was the mysterious prisoner in a velvet mask who died in the Bastille at the beginning of the eighteenth century, others that he had suffered solely because he had ventured to cast his eyes upon the mistress of the King. But the story of the greatness and fall of the Minister is sufficiently dramatic without such embroideries. Furthermore its historical significance is considerable. Louis had made plain by a striking example that he meant what he said when he announced that he intended to be his own Prime Minister. At the same time he gave warning of the dire punishment that awaited anyone who might attempt to be other than his obsequious servant. It was the classical method of establishing a tyranny.

For the same reason Louis XIV chose his ministers from the bourgeoisie instead of the nobility and continued Richelieu's policy of depriving the aristocracy of their duties while leaving them their privileges. He also excluded ecclesiastics, "men of the red robe," like Richelieu and Mazarin, from his councils. The three principal ministers who now carried out his orders, Le Tellier, Lionne, and Colbert, who virtually replaced the man whom he had helped to destroy, were all of modest lineage.

And yet there was an element of irony in Louis's programme. For these men represented the rising social and economic class in seventeenth-century France. Whereas in England the new commercial and business classes joined and intermingled with the landed aristocracy and thus continued to govern the community through the revolutionary changes of three hundred years, in France the new class, having acquired political power and learned their strength under Louis XIV, was within three generations to fashion the revolution which destroyed the monarchy.

Colbert was made Controller-General of Finance and was also the most influential member of the new financial council. He assured the King that he intended to reform the entire financial administration and centralize it directly under the Crown. He worked laboriously and exercised close control over the mass of officials engaged in raising taxes and contracting loans. He hated the whole system of borrowing, which he considered wasteful and unproductive, and would have abolished rentes altogether if he could. With the aid of the Chamber of Justice which had tried Fouquet he examined the title deeds of many State creditors and by this means succeeded in materially reducing the national debt. He also carried out conversion operations without seriously affecting the King's credit, since Fouquet had undoubtedly paid too high an interest on loans. Also, like Sully, he managed to free much of the royal domain from mortgages and reduced the number of tax farms pledged to rentiers. He made use of statistical surveys and it has been claimed that he helped (with the King's encouragement) to create a "new scientific monarchy" instead of "a mystery of anachronisms and anomalies." Certainly his policy was a radical one, and he defied unpopularity.

Colbert was less successful in his efforts to reform methods of levying taxation. He tried to spread the burden of the taille more evenly and to modify the harsh treatment of tax collectors. He also attempted to make the salt tax more uniform. But broadly he failed to carry out any fundamental reforms in the taxation system. He checked frauds and thereby raised a bigger revenue for the Treasury; but, like Sully, he was unable to extend the burden of taxation to the privileged classes and he failed to stimulate industry by easing the impact on the labouring classes. Indeed his whole financial administration was fundamentally conservative. Its main aim was to lower the expenses of administration and thus raise the yield. And during the first years of the reign he did succeed in producing vast sums of money for the Government. This however, was during a period of peace. As soon as war broke out Colbert had again to resort to all the bad old financial expedients which had been practised immemorially and which, by discouraging business activity, violated his own economic tenets.

For Colbert believed that the national revenue could best be improved by stimulating the economic activity of the French people. He outlined his policy in a letter written to Mazarin in 1653:

> We must re-establish or create all industries, even luxury industries; a system of protection must be established by means of a customs tariff; trade and traders must be organised into guilds; financial hindrances which burden the people must be lightened; transport of commodities by sea and land must be restored; colonies must be developed and commercially bound to France; all barriers between France and India must be broken down; the navy must be strengthened in order to afford protection to merchant ships.

In the interests of commerce, therefore, Colbert imposed prohibitive tariff duties, particularly on Dutch goods, although he also dreamed of simplifying the existing systems of external and internal customs duties. And not only did he employ this negative means of helping national industries but he also took positive steps to introduce and nurture infant industries and a create a merchant navy.

Colbert's economic policy, which envisaged a paternal

State assisting and protecting native manufacturers and merchants while shutting out imports by laws and prohibitions, comprised all the vices of crude Protectionism. Usually in the late Middle Ages this form of State policy was modified by smuggling and licensing; in modern times it has been offset by international commercial treaties. But an unadulterated and strictly enforced protectionist policy must spell either the destruction of all foreign trade or lead to war. Colbert's policy, and especially his prohibitive tariff imposed on Dutch imports in 1667, contributed and indeed was meant to contribute to war. The logic of this policy should at least have been the freeing of internal trade from those local customs duties which have long been the fiscal curse of France. Colbert certainly made an attempt to modify and unify them, but he failed to reduce them, largely because he feared the consequent loss of revenue to the King. A wiser aspect of his commercial policy was the encouragement which he gave to shipping and to trading between France and her colonies. Unfortunately he tried to expand trade with the colonies entirely through the instrumentality of monopolist companies. In spite of the drastic means which he used to obtain subscriptions for these companies, the two most important of them, the West India and East India companies, failed to attract sufficient support, fell into debt, and gradually faded away. Colbert learned by painful experience that merchants and colonists were more likely to achieve prosperity by being left alone than by being minutely directed by the Government.

One valuable form of assistance was nevertheless provided by Colbert for French overseas trade—his assistance to shipbuilding. He created a merchant navy and provided adequate men-of-war for escort duties. He also improved and overhauled the French ports. In 1668 he became Secretary of State for the Navy and in this capacity helped to give France a fleet which could challenge comparison with those of England and Holland. He improved the conditions of service and laid Europe under contribution for shipbuilders and naval architects. Even his unsparing exertions, however, could not make France the supreme naval power in a few years.

Colbert neglected no means to introduce new industries and revive old ones in France. His chief measures were to induce experienced foreign workers to settle in France. He gave orders to the French ambassadors and other representatives abroad to search out skilled operatives and offer them good terms to work in France. Germans and Swedes came to build up the metal industries and to work mines; Dutchmen were employed on textiles, Venetians in a glass industry, while other Italians helped to revive the silk manufactures of Lyons. In spite of the King's disapproval of luxurious living (except for his Court) Colbert did much to develop luxury industries, especially lace-making. But probably Colbert's most notable action was to revive the manufacture of tapestries which had been started in the reign of Henry IV, and finally he acquired for the State the Gobelins business, which became famous throughout Europe.

French industry undoubtedly expanded during the reign of Louis XIV; Paris became Europe's centre of art and magnificence, while many provincial towns flourished and French goods acquired a world market. But it may well have been that this prosperity occurred in spite of and not because of the paternal care of the Government. State support tended to become State interference, and the elaborate mediæval guild regulations imposed by Colbert on industry were on the whole discouraging to enterprise. At a later stage in the reign, when Louis XIV adopted a policy of religious intolerance, the foreign workers who had been brought in at heavy expense were driven out of the country and the increased taxation needed in wartime hampered industrial progress. A well-meaning system of inspection and regulation added to the general harrying of French industry by the Government.

The best assistance which Colbert was to afford to industry was his improvement of the long-neglected internal system of communications. Riverways were developed and canals were built. These also benefited agriculture, but otherwise Colbert did little to help France's principal industry. Like all extreme protectionists, he was frightened of being obliged to buy wheat abroad. Consequently, to avoid famine when there were bad harvests he imposed restrictions upon the movement of crops, which forced down the price of wheat. Being a water drinker himself he failed to acknowledge the importance of the grape. He showed more concern over the silkworm. He also cared for the forests of France and for her horses. But, as always, the French peasant was compelled to shoulder the main burden of the taxes, while not profiting from the subsidies which were lavished upon infant industries and upon the skilled workmen who came from abroad.

A prodigious worker himself, Colbert's ideal was a society which accumulated wealth by the sweat of its brow and poured its surplus into the national treasury. He was in many respects a puritan in his outlook who would perhaps have been more at home in contemporary England than in the proud and martial court of Louis XIV. He openly expressed his hatred of the Roman Catholic priests and monks who, he considered, were anti-social unproductive workers and by their charitable actions encouraged idleness in others. His austere attitude to rentiers and to the wine industry further exemplified the solemnity of his economic approach. He would have liked to compel the French people to make their country rich beyond measure by unstinting labour from the cradle to the grave. He had a wrong notion of his fellow-countrymen.

It has sometimes been said that Colbert offered Louis XIV an alternative policy to that which he actually followed, that he told the King that he could make France supreme through commercial activity alone and could lead her to the pinnacle of world supremacy in peace and not by war. There is little to justify this dramatic and simplified account of French history. No one in the seventeenth century thought otherwise than in terms of constant national wars, and Colbert's own programme of aggressive protectionism could in any case have been enforced only at the point of the sword. Indeed Professor Heckscher has claimed that Colbert's form of State economic policy was warlike in its characteristics and in its objectives. The truth is that Colbert realized—and the King himself recognized—that after twenty-five years of war and after the nation had reached the verge of bankruptcy the country needed a breathing-space. Before the French armed forces could take the world by storm, a substantial war chest and a militant economic policy were necessary. Louis XIV himself recorded in 1661 that although he was impatient to acquire a glorious reputation, he realized that he must first promote a measure of internal reform. Colbert as Minister of Finance (in effect, if not in name) merely obeyed his orders just as his other Ministers, Lionne and Louvois, fulfilled his wishes in the conduct of foreign affairs. The King was throughout, as he wished to be, the master.

There is only one sense in which, as some historians have asserted, Colbert made an "offer" to Louis XIV of an alternative policy to that which was indeed followed by him. In a memorandum he proposed to the King that he should aim at attaining the commercial supremacy of the world by destroying France's successful rivals, Holland and England. But the King considered that commerce was a low and ignoble form of activity, and he hated the sea; he would have made a seasick admiral and much preferred to be an imposing general. The King's driving motives in foreign policy were in fact well disclosed by two revealing passages in his *Memoirs* in which he speaks to his son about the Emperor. He went out of his way to stress his contempt, and therefore his obvious jealousy, of the Habsburg ruler. Charlemagne, he announced, had been the only real ruler of Europe—and the King of France must be his successor. He therefore "laboured to ruin the Emperor's credit further and to destroy that authority which the House of Austria had established in Germany over the centuries." Though there were many and deeper causes, Louis's overweening love of self-glorification helped to perpetuate the enmity of France and Germany.

In pursuit of the policy of glorification Louis XIV made good use of the strong position in which he had been placed by historical circumstances and by the activities of his predecessors. His knowledge of foreign affairs was wide if not deep, and in the early years of his reign he had a just notion of how far he dared go without provoking war. In October 1661 a dispute between the French and Spanish ambassadors for precedence at the Court of St. James gave Louis an opportunity to humiliate his father-in-law, the King of Spain: the Spanish ambassador in France was obliged to apologize before the whole Court. In the summer of 1662, on the King's instructions, a quarrel was deliberately picked by the French ambassador in Rome. The Pope apologized for the behaviour of his Corsican guards, who had fired at the carriage of the ambassador's wife, and gave expression to his regrets in a concrete form by permitting a pyramid to be erected in Rome with an inscription indicating the papal sorrow. Similarly the French monarch objected to his warships being obliged to dip their flags to the English. Charles II ordered his admirals to salute the French flag in Mediterranean waters but added a secret rider that they should avoid doing so wherever possible.

In consequence of these incidents Sir William Temple in 1663 saluted this "great comet which has risen rapidly —the King of France who wants not merely to be gazed at but to be admired by the whole world." Under the impact of his easy diplomatic successes the King sought further and more substantial gains. His head swelled and he prepared to filch territory from the Habsburgs. In preparation for this end he purchased Dunkirk and Mardyke from the impecunious English King and entered into alliances with the Electors of Saxony and Brandenburg. He lent his secret support to the King of Portugal in his efforts to throw off allegiance to Spain and promoted the marriage of Charles II of England to the unprepossessing Catherine of Braganza with her handsome dowry of Tangier and Bombay; he spoke hypocritically of "his extreme zeal for the maintenance of German liberties";

and he even in April 1662 entered into an offensive and defensive alliance with the Dutch Republic. The alliance between France and Holland was scarcely that of two true hearts but rather of neighbours who found it paid them better to come to an arrangement than to quarrel. Since both were the traditional opponents of Spain they had common interests. De Witt, who guided the fortunes of the Republic, painfully recognized the supreme power of the French monarchy, while the French King hoped to buy off Dutch opposition to French expansion to the north-east.

All Europe was now awaiting the death of the King of Spain and its inevitable consequences. As early as 1663 Louis XIV discovered a local law in Brabant—"the law of devolution"—whereby the children of a first wife succeeded to an inheritance in preference to the children of the second. The application of this law to the Spanish Netherlands (Belgium) would have meant that Louis's wife, Maria Theresa, would acquire them upon the death of her father instead of her stepbrother, the infant Charles. In September 1665 Philip IV descended into the tomb, soon after he had heard the news that the Spanish army had been decisively defeated by the Portuguese. By his will he specifically excluded his eldest daughter from any right of succession to the Spanish throne and made it clear that the Netherlands were an integral part of the Spanish Empire. His devotion to the unity of Spain and his fears of Louis XIV's ambitions were to be transmitted to his weakling son Charles, whose death was regarded as an impending event by European diplomatists for the next thirty years.

Meanwhile, Louis was faced with an embarrassing situation. Early in 1665 England and Holland went to war and the Dutch demanded that the French King should fulfil the obligations undertaken in the treaty of 1662. Louis long hesitated. When Philip IV died his inclination was immediately to make war on Spain, and the temptation to find an excuse to avoid keeping his promises to the Dutch was strong. He also considered the possibility of waging a double war. His interests and his personal preferences favoured a land war; he did not consider it proper to expose his own person to the caprices of the ocean. However, he reluctantly declared war on England in January 1666, hoping to bring it to an amiable conclusion as quickly as possible and at the same time to complete his preparations for an assault on Spain. Louis did little to help the Dutch, but the Dutch helped themselves and in June 1667 concluded the Treaty of Breda with England. A month earlier Louis attacked the Spanish Netherlands.

By untiring diplomacy with the aid of his Foreign Minister, Lionne, Louis had succeeded in virtually isolating Spain; the alliance with Portugal had been renewed in March 1667, Holland owed a debt of gratitude, the German princes and the English King had been bribed to support the French interest. Although the young Emperor Leopold, who married a daughter of Philip IV's second wife, was anxious to support his Spanish relatives, an attempt by the Imperialist diplomatist Lisola to create an anti-French coalition failed. Marshal Turenne with 30,000 French soldiers crossed the Somme and the King set up his headquarters at Amiens. The King, on the dubious basis of his wife's hereditary rights, laid claim to large parts of Flanders and Luxembourg. The Spanish Queen Mother offered to submit the French demands to a conference, but in the end war broke out. This was known as the War of Devolution or, as the French preferred to call it, the War of the Queen's Rights. A series of carefully planned French victories followed. The frontier towns of Tournai, Douai, and Courtrai capitulated in turn. Then Lille fell, and Europe trembled. Bowing to the inevitable, the Emperor Leopold signed a secret treaty with the French King (known as the Partition Treaty of 1668) whereby on the expected approaching death of King Charles II of Spain, France was to obtain the Spanish Netherlands, Naples, Sicily, Franche-Comté (that is, that part of the old Duchy of Burgundy lying to the south-west of Alsace), the Philippines, and parts of Africa.

While two brothers-in-law thus conspired to share out

the possessions of a third brother-in-law, still a small child, the war continued under the victorious direction of Turenne and Condé. The conquest of Flanders was compared to a ceremonial march. The King took his whole Court, his Queen, and his mistresses on campaign with him and enjoyed supervising the leisurely and dignified sieges which were the fashionable mode of waging war.

The chief Minister of the United Netherlands, the Grand Pensionary de Witt, had tried to limit Louis XIV's demands upon Spain, for the last thing that he wanted was a powerful and aggressive neighbour. For Spain, as Lord Acton observed, the Netherlands were only an outlying dependency, for Holland they were a rampart. When Louis refused to compromise, de Witt proceeded to form a Triple Alliance with England and Sweden to impose restrictions upon French expansion. The Alliance was completed in January 1668, but in May Louis signed the Treaty of Aix-la-Chapelle with Spain, which brought the war to an end. By this treaty he obtained Douai, Tournai, Oudenarde, Lille, Courtrai, and other Flemish towns, but agreed to restore Franche-Comté to Spain. It is still disputed how far the creation of the Triple Alliance compelled Louis to end the war. There is no doubt that the decision to make peace at this stage reflected that mixture of prudence with daring which the King had so far shown in his whole conduct of foreign affairs, for Turenne had been anxious to continue the war and to push the French frontier as far forward as Antwerp. Moreover, the Treaty of Partition with Leopold promised rich gains for France in the near future which ought not to be jeopardized. On the other hand, the hostility of the Protestant Powers was a factor in the King's calculations—and Louis was never to forgive or forget this action of the Dutch Republic.

One curious episode in the foreign policy of Louis XIV in the years 1661 to 1668 concerns Lorraine. Lorraine was a separate principality and its Duke offered to cede his estates to the French Crown in return for the right to retain the income from them. This negotiation broke down over relatively unimportant questions of princely precedence. Thus, although France had gained Alsace early in the reign, she failed, when excellent opportunities presented themselves, to acquire either Lorraine or Franche Comté, the possession of which would have cleared the communications between France and Alsace. True, Franche Comté was to be conquered later, but—despite many subsequent fruitless efforts by Louis XIV—France did not obtain Lorraine until 1735. To these solid acquisitions, which France might then have had almost for the asking, Louis preferred the grand hopes of wide empire embodied in his secret treaty with the Emperor Leopold. Henceforward the whole of his policy was to be dictated by the lure of gain held out by the approaching break-up of the Spanish monarchy: Naples, Antwerp, Madrid even, all these Louis hoped might become part of the realm of a new Charlemagne in which Bourbon should humiliate Habsburg once and for ever. What might not now be achieved by a brave and experienced army and by accomplished diplomacy, directed by a fine Italian hand? These paths of glory were in the end only to lead to the brink of disaster for France.

Chapter 4

The Court of Versailles

THE SCENE OF Louis XIV's chief pleasures and, later, of his labours was the palace of Versailles which (in the words of Mme de Motteville) was the "place he designed for his magnificence in order to show by its adornment what a great king can do when he spares nothing to satisfy his wishes." In abandoning Saint-Germain and Fontainebleau, the traditional country homes of the French monarchs, in favour of Versailles, he flew in the face of nature. Versailles, wrote Saint-Simon caustically, was "the saddest and most ungrateful of all places, without a view, without woods or water or good soil, for it all stood upon shifting sands or marshland which inevitably made the air bad." The estate had originally been acquired by Louis XIII from a forbear of Cardinal Retz and was used by him for hunting and the pursuit of his chaste love affairs. A charming palace, consisting of a main building and two wings, was built in 1634 and Louis XIV passed many happy hours there as a boy. This palace was nicknamed the "little house of cards"; it contained simple furnishings, Brussels tapestries, and a painting of the siege of La Rochelle, and was pleasantly set amid a wood, ponds, and fields.

It seems almost certain that Louis was inspired to transform this modest estate into halls and gardens which should adequately reflect the royal magnificence by the visit that he paid to Nicholas Fouquet's lovely home at Vaux-le-Vicomte on the eve of that statesman's fall. For the work which was set on foot at Versailles was carried out almost entirely by Fouquet's former employees, the architect, Louis Le Vaux, the painter, Charles Le Brun, and the landscape gardener, André Le Notre, while the entertainments there were to be provided mainly by the artists whom Fouquet had discovered, the comedian Molière and the Italian musician, Lully. During the years

1661–1668 terraces, gardens, fountains, stables, and a swan lake were added to the amenities of the royal estate. A cherished addition was the Orangery, a vaulted and arcaded building furnished with over twelve hundred orange trees specially grown in nursery gardens. Terraces, balconies, classical temples, and sculptures were designed to set off the ordered beauty of the gardens; the statues were first chiselled from stone but later gave way to marble. In 1663 work was begun on a zoo which was intended to be "the most magnificent palace of animals in the whole world." No effort or expense was spared. Trees were uprooted in the farthest corners of France to be replanted in the glades of Versailles. Vast numbers of workmen were employed to construct a drainage system and to induce the waters to spurt lavishly from the fountains into the artificial gardens hewn from the former wasteland. It is true that the workmen who dug the canals to carry water from the river Eure to the fountains died by thousands of marsh fever. Such unpleasant incidents were concealed. The carts moved the dead from the local hospital by night: "this sad procession was hidden so as not to frighten the workmen or expose the bad air of this favourite without merit." So wrote Mme de Sévigné in a letter to her cousin, who replied stiffly: "I do not know why Versailles is called a favourite without merit . . . Kings can by the power of money give the earth a different form from that which it has been given by nature —but the quality of the water and air is not in their power."

Colbert, who since 1664 held among his offices that of Superintendant of Buildings and was a man of some taste and judgment, made a brave but vain protest against the King's extravagances. He argued that the Louvre, which was then being extended and rebuilt, was a far more worthy symbol of the royal greatness. But the King disliked Paris and went there as seldom as he could. He obstinately devoted his personal care and his love of detail to the embellishment of Versailles. Here he was at his best and his most gracious. When the Venetian ambassador visited the palace in 1671, the King himself delightedly showed him around the gardens and volubly explained the projected improvements. At a later period, in 1689, Mme de Sévigné, who lived on the edge of the Court but not in it, was invited to a performance of Racine's play *Esther* by the younger daughters of the nobility and recorded what was no doubt an everyday incident.

"The King (she related) came towards our seats and turned around and addressed me saying: 'Madame, I am certain that you have enjoyed yourself.' I replied calmly: 'Sire, I was delighted; I cannot express what I felt.' The King said: 'Racine is a great dramatist.' I said to him: 'Sire, that is true; but in truth these young girls have also plenty of spirit; they entered into their parts as if they had been born actresses.' He said to me: 'Ah! that is very true.' And then his Majesty moved away and left me the object of envy." Even Saint-Simon, whose *Memoirs* are an acid indictment of the whole reign of Louis XIV and who denied that the King had either ability or good taste, had to admit that he was the soul of charm and courtesy. He had too a remarkable memory for people and cast a perspicacious eye over every detail of his Court and public affairs, although he never committed himself on personal matters if he could avoid doing so.

In 1668, after his triumph at the Treaty of Aix-la-Chapelle, Louis decided that Versailles should henceforward house his Court and Councils and that his servants and ministers should live and work there. Until then it had been a country palace where the royal hospitality could occasionally be displayed in its most luxurious vein. Here in 1664 the King had given a party which he called "Pleasures of the Enchanted Island" in honour of Mlle de La Vallière; there were balls, plays, music, and fireworks which turned night into day. Four years later he organized a similar fête dedicated to love and glory and to the Marquise de Montespan, who had replaced Mlle de La Vallière as *maitresse-en-titre*. But on these occasions there was scarcely room for all the guests, servants, entertainers and hangers-on who had to be accommodated.

So the decision was taken to rebuild and extend the palace and to construct a town by its side.

Work was begun on the new buildings, which were called the Château Neuf, in the autumn of 1668. The architect was again Louis Le Vaux and he was strictly ordered by the King not to destroy his father's palace but to envelop it with new buildings in the "Louis XIV manner" with columns, pilasters, and high white façades. Le Vaux died in 1670 and the plan was brought to its completion by his pupil, François Dorbay. Eight years later another architect, Jules Hardouin Mansard, added to Le Vaux's work by constructing the famous Hall of Mirrors (finished in 1684). Two gorgeous staircases were erected in the wings on either side of the original palace leading to the royal apartments. These apartments were wonderfully decorated and painted, while the tapestries were the finest products of the Gobelins factory. The symbol for the whole palace was Apollo, the Sun God:

> It should be noticed first of all (wrote a contemporary) that as the Sun is the King's emblem and as the poets confound the sun with Apollo, there is nothing in the superb palace which does not bear relation to that deity; thus the statues and ornaments are not put into haphazard positions but are related either to the sun or to the particular spots where they are placed.

Some of the statues represented the fruits of the earth, some the winds, some the months of the year—all the products or the handmaids of the Sun.

At the same time that the new palace was built the gardens were extended and decorated with new marvels such as a labyrinth, a new menagerie, a Grand Canal, and beds filled with Provençal flowers. The King's desires were not even sated by all these costly works of art. Other palaces were built in the neighbourhood of Versailles Park: the Trianon, "a palace of marble, jasper, and porphyry," amid perfumed gardens where the monarch entertained his ladies; Clagny, a lovely house and park, built for one lady, Mme de Montespan. Finally, the King sought

for himself a country house where he might retire from
the crowd of courtiers, and ordered his architects to find
a site near Versailles "with a good view, water, and trees";
and on such a site they built the palace of Marly, which,
according to Saint-Simon, cost as much as Versailles itself and may well have been as beautiful.

At Versailles Louis XIV conferred his patronage on the
artists and men of letters whose work has shed enduring
lustre upon his reign. It must not, however, be imagined
that this was a sudden flowering of French genius. Before
Louis took over the personal direction of government,
giants had made their appearance: Nicholas Poussin,
whom William Hazlitt called the most poetical of all
painters (he, however, lived almost all his life in Rome);
Pierre Corneille, author of romantic and powerful tragedies; Blaise Pascal, mathematician, thinker, and mystic,
whose witty and polished writings were impregnated with
the spirit of the Middle Ages; and, above all, René Descartes, a philosopher whose influence was to dominate
French thought. Colbert, who in virtue of his office of
Superintendant of Buildings functioned as a kind of
Minister of Fine Arts, gathered a crowd of artists and
writers under his wing for the purpose of officially glorify-
ing the Sun King.

Colbert did not confine his patronage to French artists
but invited leading men from abroad to contribute their
talents, just as he brought skilled foreign artisans to revive
French industries. Bernini, architect of the Vatican, was
fetched from Rome to advise on the design of the Louvre,
although his designs were not accepted; Huygens, astrono-
mer, scientist, and inventor of clocks, came from Holland;
and each year huge crates of sculptures were transported
to France from various parts of Italy.

Charles Le Brun was the favourite artistic adviser of
Colbert and of the King. Partly trained in Rome, Le Brun
was fondest of grand motifs in the classical manner. He
was a mediocre painter but a prolific decorator and a
skilled designer in a heavy and heroic manner; his successors were Pierre Mignard and later Antoine Coypel and

Charles de La Fosse. In portraiture Mignard also established the tradition of painting court beauties as goddesses, which was carried on by Largillière and Rigaud. The better painters of the reign were, however, not these pompous flatterers and academicians, but men like Claude de Lorraine, who, like Poussin, lived in Rome, Van der Meulen, a Belgian, and in later years Antoine Watteau (1684–1721), who was influenced by Rubens and the Flemish school. In Watteau's paintings idealized scenes of Parisian society were modified by a genuine appreciation of the French countryside. In Coysevox and Girardin, Watteau had contemporaries who were sculptors of striking busts and allegorical groups. But the painters and sculptors of the last period of the reign owed little to official patronage. Louvois, the War Minister, who succeeded Colbert as Superintendant of Buildings, announced that "he preferred a good copy of a polished marble to an antique with a broken nose," and his successors singularly failed to encourage genuine artists, while in any case they had pitifully small budgets for patronage.

Lully ruled music as Le Brun ruled painting. In 1672 it was forbidden to give performances accompanied by more than two airs and two instruments without his written permission. The King was something of a musician himself (as was his rival, the Emperor Leopold) and the gardens of Versailles were constantly filled with concerts, ballets, and operas. Lully was an Italian but in Lalande France produced a composer of ability who wrote symphonies for the King's suppers.

But it is above all in the fields of prose and poetry that the age of Louis XIV was supreme. Lashed by the caustic wit of the critic Boileau, "the Lawgiver of Parnassus," French writers eschewed the artificial and precious and prided themselves on the polish, clarity, and economical quality of their prose. La Rochefoucauld unburdened himself of deadly if overrated epigrams in his "terrible little book" of *Maxims,* which went through six editions between 1666 and 1678; de Retz, that rare and entertaining liar, Mme de Motteville, and the King's cousin, Mlle de Montpensier, wrote enduring and lively volumes of memoirs. La Bruyère wrote supple essays containing moral reflections and literary criticism. Bossuet, an orthodox Catholic, a master of rhetorical prose (in the words of Lytton Strachey) "saw all round his age but not beyond it." But perhaps the most typical writer of the reign was Mme de Sévigné, whose voluminous and absorbing letters to her daughter faithfully mirror her age.

The leading poets of the time were La Fontaine (1621–1695) and Jean Racine (1639–1699). La Fontaine, the son of a forestry official, had invented a novel form of literary entertainment in his poetic fables, which became the rage of the Court. Although he in the end paid lip service to the fashions of the century, he was at heart an epicurean and a vagabond who regarded death as "the end of a fine day." Racine, on the other hand, was in his later years a devout Christian and a bold defender of an unorthodox form of Catholicism. His tragedies were intense and compact poetic dramas saturated in the theme of love. They had an immediate and widespread vogue and, in the history of French literature, they have something of the place of Shakespeare's plays in our literature.

Racine's contemporary dramatist Molière (1622–1673) was, like most of the other writers, a middle-class genius raised to the heights of success by the patronage of the Court. In his comedies he criticized in a witty and subtle fashion the social habits of his day. In his most remarkable play *Tartuffe* he pilloried not merely hypocrisy but, by implication, Christianity itself. Suffering from ill-health and an unhappy marriage, some of his bitter satires narrowly approach the frontier of tragedy. All his drama lay in his characters and dialogue, rather than in the situations. His versatility, his knowledge of humanity, and his extraordinary compound of humour and melancholy make him one of the outstanding figures in the history not merely of French but of world literature.

The reign of Louis XIV also saw the birth of the modern novel. The history of French fiction was then already old, including, as it did, the gargantuan tales of

Rabelais and culminating in the work of the versatile cripple Paul Scarron. We have seen how Louis XIV and his first love, Marie Mancini, used to read romances together; such works were florid and lengthy, Mme de Scudéry producing, for example, a novel called *Clélie* in twenty volumes. But Mme de La Fayette (it is remarkable how women's names punctuate the history of novel writing) was the first French novelist to tell stories that really concerned themselves with human motives and living characters. Her best-known novel was called *The Princess of Cleves* (published in 1667) and is based on the writer's own experience at the Court of Louis XIV where she had been the friend alike of the cynical La Rochefoucauld and talented Mme de Sévigné.

In the early years of the King's period of personal rule many of these writers and artists were lavishly patronized. A small committee was formed by Colbert to encourage and subsidize artists and the production of works of art; historical research and scientific investigations were also promoted by the State. Although one of the duties of this committee was to give pensions to foreigners, Colbert was anxious to foster purely French works of art and literature. Members of the Royal Academy were made to clock in regularly every day in order to compile a definitive dictionary of the French language. An Academy of Sciences was incorporated in 1666 and lodged in the Louvre, and the Royal Academy of Painters and Sculptors also obtained privileges and quarters in the Louvre. An Academy of Architects was founded in 1671. These academicians worked out careful rules for design based upon such classical authors as Vitruvius, and despised those "Gothic barbarities" which are the glory of French architecture. In general, academies and schools of art had a heyday during the reign of Louis XIV and spread outwards from Paris to the provinces.

It has sometimes been stated (notably by Lytton Strachey) that this splendid period in French literature and art owed its existence and development to the patronage of the King and its public to the Court of Versailles.

But it is difficult to substantiate this claim except in a limited sense. The French "Augustan" age began before Louis XIV took over the personal direction of the administration in 1661; Descartes, whose translucent prose induced French writers to turn away from the over-elaborate style of the French Precious School, published his *Discourse on Method* in 1637. Corneille's tragedies and comedies, which were models both to Racine and to Molière, were mostly written before 1661. Molière's *Precieuses Ridicules* was written in 1659. Moreover the man who had patronized and encouraged Molière, La Fontaine, and many other great writers and artists was not Louis XIV or Colbert but Nicholas Fouquet, a discerning Mæcenas, whom the King had overthrown and disgraced out of jealousy. The royal bounty extended less to the support of rising artists than to the payment of work by those who had already arrived. And the royal generosity was not sustained. The budget for the arts fell from a height of fifteen million livres to 1,200,000 livres at the end of the reign. And just as at the beginning of Louis XIV's reign Fouquet was the most appreciative patron, at the end of the reign it was the Parisian bourgeoisie and not the officials of Versailles or Marly who assisted artists and writers of real talent.

Indeed in many ways Louis XIV's patronage proved actually damaging to the output of original creative work. The academies tended to stifle unorthodoxy. The emphasis placed upon decoration stultified painting, and it was not until French painters broke away from the influence of Raphael and the Caracci and turned for inspiration to Rubens and the Flemish School that an original talent presented itself. Similarly in the realm of literature, men of genius were corrupted by the syco-phantic adulation that they were expected to contribute to the royal glory. Even the orthodox Bishop Bossuet was not guiltless of servility, and that penetrating critic Boileau made a fool of himself when he tried to write an heroic ode in honour of the King's conquest of Namur. La Bruyère threw a revealing light upon the limitations which the government of Louis XIV imposed upon writers when he stated that "important topics were forbidden." It was not until the last years of the reign that a brave and brilliant author in Archbishop Fénelon dared to attack autocracy and breathe a spirit of political liberalism which pointed the way across the wastes of Louis XV's reign towards the French Revolution.

The King had almost oriental ideas on the subject of women, and Versailles was his harem. After his mother, who had some restraining influence upon him, died, he ceased to keep up appearances. When members of the Parliament of Paris presented themselves to commiserate with the King on the passing of the Queen Mother in January 1666, Mlle de la Vallière, as well as the Queen, was there to receive the deputation. The Queen had borne the King a son in 1661, who was the only one of her seven children to survive childhood. Mlle de la Vallière gave him a daughter in 1666 and was to present him with a son in 1667. All his sons were named Louis. The Queen had grown used to Louise de La Vallière, who was a pleasant enough young lady and had indeed become friendly with her. But the death of the Queen Mother brought into being a whole host of rivals to her. The hopeful aspirants consulted fortune tellers, witches, and even poisoners whose advice on how to get rid of unwanted husbands was freely sought by a fashionable and credulous society. One of the best-known of this criminal class was a Mme Montvoisin or "La Voisin," who had a large clientèle, a clamorous family, and no conscience. Among the young ladies who consulted her and no doubt partook of her black magic and black masses was the Marquise de Montespan.

Mme de Montespan, with fair hair, big blue eyes, and a perfect figure, was very beautiful, entertaining, generous, and "as wicked as the devil himself." She succeeded in winning the King, to whom she bore two sons and two daughters (1673-1678) and for some years she exercised a real hold over him, even though he apparently knew of her dubious past and her dealings with the criminal classes of Paris. Louise de La Vallière, when she realized that she had lost the King, whom she sincerely loved, attempted to retire into a convent and do penance. The King, however, sent Colbert after her and brought her back to Court for another three years. She then again returned to a convent, where in 1675 she cut off her hair and took her vows as Louise de La Miséricorde. The new nun was frequently visited by her old friends from the Court. One day the Queen paid her a call in the company of Mme de Montespan, who enquired if she was pleased with what she had done. "No," she replied, "I am not pleased, but I am content." When her day was done Mme de Montespan also retired to a convent, where she ended her life in a most exemplary manner.

To look after the children whom she had by the King, Mme de Montespan took as their governess the widow of the poet Paul Scarron, better known as Mme de Maintenon, whom the King came to admire for her sympathy and her intelligence. At first more dashing rivals to Mme de Montespan presented themselves, the cunning Mme de Soubise, Mme de Ludres, a canoness with a German accent, and Mlle de Fontanges, of whom it was said that she was "as beautiful as an angel and as stupid as a basket." Mme de Montespan, "la belle des belles," as her friend Mme de Sévigné called her, recaptured her positions intact against all these spirited attacks. But Mme de Maintenon was able to offer the King qualities which Mme de Montespan could not rival, and when in 1680 the Voisin affair became public and the King could no longer ignore the criminal associations of his mistress, the field was clear for Mme de Maintenon. Six months after the death of Maria Theresa, in January 1684, the King secretly married her.

Louis XIV was forty-six when he married Mme de Maintenon, and henceforward he abandoned all illegitimate love affairs and followed a domestic life of almost middle-class respectability. Mme de Maintenon was Queen in a far more real sense than poor Maria Theresa ever was. It is, however, doubtful how far she was conscious of the honour that was done her. She was in a constant state of boredom, finding the ceremonies she was compelled to attend wearying in the extreme. She was a born governess and school teacher, and found her deepest happiness in the school for young girls which she supervised at the village of Saint-Cyr. One day she told her elegant pupils that "when the time came for them to be married, they would find it was no laughing matter." Whatever her thoughts may have been, she was a loyal and devoted wife, modest in her demands and wise in her choice of friends. She gave the King comfort and happiness.

Saint-Cyr was only an occasional interlude and source of escape for Mme de Maintenon. The King expected to find her wherever he was. When the long day's duties were finished and dinner eaten the royal couple would seat themselves on opposite sides of the fireplace, he at a table loaded with papers, she reading or doing tapestry work. A modest supper of meat and fruit was brought in at ten o'clock. Then if Mme de Maintenon was tired, she would be undressed by two of her maids in front of the King and his Minister.

Thus Louis himself lived a private life not dissimilar from that of his more famous subjects. First, he sowed his wild oats; then he plunged into a period of almost reckless pleasure; and if in the end he could not retire to a monastery to expiate the sins impressed upon him by his confessors, to be married to the religious and melancholy Mme de Maintenon may have been an effective substitute.

The King treated the presence of the greater nobles at Versailles and Fontainebleau as a parade, and if he found any were missing he enquired sharply about the reasons for their absence. But the function of the nobility was almost totally ornamental. They were strictly excluded from all ministerial duties and from the royal counsels, and they were not allowed to do honest work of any kind. The only thing they were permitted to do was to fight, and consequently the more energetic among them pressed the King to go to war at frequent intervals. At the same time, although they were exempt from taxation, the French nobles had expensive estates to keep up and many onerous ceremonial functions to fulfil. The King seems deliberately to have encouraged them to indulge in the most extravagant luxuries. Thus, unless they were lucky enough to make a rich marriage, many of them were in due course ruined. A report made by the Intendants on Colbert's behalf disclosed that poverty was almost general among the nobility and that the main cause of their debts was the heavy cost of life at Court.

One cannot escape the conclusion that it was the intention of Louis XIV to bring about the ruin of the French nobility "of the Sword" in a way which had not been contemplated even by Richelieu. Louis never forgot the powerful lessons he had learnt during the civil wars of his youth. He wreaked his revenge upon the city of Paris by building Versailles, and upon the nobility, who had dared to raise their swords against his mother, by turning his Court into what was in effect a luxurious gambling-den in which the croupier always won. But it was not only the nobility but the whole monarchic system that the King injured by the creation of Versailles. Through building an all-embracing palace and an artificial city on a wasteland and living and working in it, surrounded chiefly by servile ministers and idle courtiers, Louis XIV cut himself off from his people and, like Philip II of Spain, was unable to compensate by hours of unremitting toil at his desk for lack of contact with the realities of the everyday life of his subjects. As that profound and witty French historian, M. Lavisse, observed:

The great events of the reign are not always those which at once spring to the mind. The establishment at Versailles was more important and had graver consequences than any of Louis XIV's wars or all of his wars put together.

Chapter 5

Shipwreck of a System

LOUIS XIV WAS NOT WILLING to accept the limitations imposed upon his expansionist foreign policy by the opposition of the Dutch Republic. The affront offered to the glory of the absolute monarchy by the diplomatic resistance of the upstart merchants of Holland, whom he had befriended, seriously perturbed the King; the desire of his chief minister, Colbert, to ruin Dutch foreign trade—an ambition which had found expression in the prohibitive tariffs imposed by him on Dutch imports in 1667—was no doubt an important factor making for war; but the main reason why, after the conclusion of the Treaty of Aix-la-Chapelle, Louis prepared to attack the United Netherlands was unquestionably that they stood directly in the path of his territorial aims.

The decision of the French King to overthrow the Dutch Republic meant a reversal of French foreign policy as practised by Richelieu and Mazarin, and in thrusting the Protestant Dutch (together, in later years, with the Protestant English) into the arms of the Catholic Habsburgs Louis made a fatal, if not exceptional, mistake: for aggressive Powers in Europe have invariably created surprising coalitions against them. Thus it came about, as the French historian, Mignet, wrote, that "the old political system of France suffered shipwreck in Holland."

As his habit was, the French monarch made ready carefully and completely for his new war. "The years between 1668 and 1672," wrote the biographer of the French War Minister, Louvois, "were years of preparation; when Lionne was labouring with all his might to find allies, Colbert money, and Louvois soldiers for Louis."

The principal achievement of French diplomacy during these years was the destruction of the Triple Alliance of England, Sweden, and the United Netherlands. Pomponne, the able French ambassador in Sweden, whom Louis appointed as Lionne's successor when he died in 1671, managed to detach the Swedes from the alliance by a secret treaty of April 1672, in which they promised to oppose any German ruler who attempted to interfere in the coming war against Holland. Two months later an even more valuable treaty was signed with Charles II of England. By the secret Treaty of Dover Louis XIV and Charles II agreed "to humble the pride of the States-General and to destroy the power of a people which has not only shown ingratitude to those who have helped it to create its republic but has had the insolence to set itself up as a sovereign arbiter among other states." The English contribution to this end was to be 6,000 infantry and sixty men-of-war and the English share of the spoils of the expected victory was to be the island of Walcheren, Sluys, and Cadsand. Charles II also agreed in this treaty to declare himself at an unspecified date to be a Roman Catholic. A truncated version of the treaty, omitting the conversion clause, was later signed by the non-Catholic members of Charles II's council. The French King cemented the new alliance with England by the provision of subsidies and a French mistress for Charles II.

French diplomacy also made excellent progress in Germany. With the exception of the Hohenzollern Elector of Brandenburg, who allied himself with the Dutch, all the German princes accepted subsidies and guaranteed their neutrality or offered their assistance to the French. The daughter of the powerful Elector of Bavaria was betrothed to Louis XIV's heir, the Dauphin, then aged nine. The Elector of Cologne promised 18,000 troops for use against the Dutch. Finally the pusillanimous Emperor Leopold, who was at the time distracted by unrest in Hungary, signed a treaty of neutrality with France on condition that the coming war did not obtrude across the imperial frontiers.

These were all outstanding triumphs for French diplomacy. It was generally agreed that at this date the diplomatic service of Louis XIV was easily the most dexterous in the world, that it occupied the same leading place in seventeenth-century European politics as Italian diplomacy had held in earlier times. It has often been emphasized that the French King himself was directly responsible for policy—in the words of a contemporary Italian: "he was in no way dominated by his ministers and never was a prince less governed." That is true; but one must distinguish between actual responsibility for taking final decisions and the formulation and execution of the plans. Foreign affairs were discussed and decided in the small Council of State (which has already been described); the execution of policy was largely in the hands of the Foreign Minister (literally Secretary of State for Foreign Affairs) who drafted letters and dispatches for the royal signature. Our knowledge is not complete enough to enable us to say how far Louis himself originated lines of policy. An informed German observer declared that Louis was not a genius of that high order who is capable of reaching decisions on his own and carrying through plans unassisted and that he never really possessed a balanced view on foreign affairs. Still, the point is that he did not shirk taking the final decisions and accepting responsibility for them—and he insisted upon being consulted over all important dispatches and seeing all the relevant documents. Louis never slavishly followed the advice of his Minister or of the majority of his Council in foreign affairs, as he was wont to do in military matters.

Louis perfected the diplomatic machinery which he had inherited and personally selected his ministers and ambassadors, if not always with the happiest results. He demanded that all his foreign representatives should keep him informed personally and at length of the situation in the countries where they were stationed. In some cases he even organized secret negotiations without letting his official advisers know about them. The success both of his secret and of his open diplomacy was due to the number and quality of the French representatives abroad. In Italy and in Germany France had more diplomatic agents than any other nation, while frequent use was also made of ambassadors extraordinary. The diplomatic career was thrown open alike to lawyers, soldiers, and clergy; and although they were not always well treated by the authorities at home and their pay tended to come through irregularly, they were a conscientious and capable set of men. So too were the officials of Versailles, as may be seen from the detail and perspicacity of the instructions which were provided for French representatives abroad on taking up their appointments.

At home the Secretary of State for Foreign Affairs was assisted by a large staff of officials, decoders, propagandists, and archivists. Abroad he could rely not only upon the ambassadors and ministers but upon a widespread network of special agents who undertook secret negotiations or provided intelligence. Most of the peace negotiations were set on foot initially by members of this latter class. Among them were frocked and unfrocked priests, international adventurers, shady ladies, and the diplomatic representatives of some of the smaller and more impecunious courts. A typical French agent was the "Abbé" Pregnani, an Italian astrologer, who was sent to the Court of Charles II of England to support the policy of the Treaty of Dover; unfortunately Charles II took him to the Newmarket races, where he lost reputation by proving incapable of forecasting the winners. Large sums of money were made available by the French Treasury in support of French diplomacy. A rain of French gold poured out on the English, Swedish, and Polish courts— a flood which dried up only in the closing years of the reign.

This elaborate diplomatic system had its faults, as will be seen, for the alliance of powerful States cannot be purchased for long and the cleverest diplomacy could not sustain a policy of aggression once it threatened the interests of the whole of Europe. Those mistakes must of course be laid at the door of the King himself, who took the final decisions. But the technique was superb and French diplomatic institutions long remained models. The example of France, wrote Professor Picavet, greatly favoured the multiplication of permanent embassies, while the French language became in the eighteenth century that of common diplomatic usage. Even when the French monarchy disappeared, the traditions of its diplomacy survived almost unimpaired.

As in the machinery of diplomacy, so in that of war, Louis XIV did not so much carry out far-reaching reforms as improve and develop the instruments which he had inherited. Louis's chief servants in the work of army reform were Sébastien Vauban and the Marquis de Louvois. Vauban was one of the real men of genius of the reign. A man of genuine inventiveness, versatility, and reformist ideas, his career embraced many sides of the nation's life; it culminated in the publication of a remarkable book which advocated the abolition of fiscal privileges and the introduction of a uniform system of taxation; for writing it he earned the royal ingratitude of disgrace after many years of faithful service. Although Louvois inherited the post of Secretary of State for War from his father, Michel Le Tellier, in 1662, his father really remained in charge of the office until 1677, and the creation of Louis XIV's army owes as much to the father as to the son. Both men were first-rate administrators.

What Le Tellier and Louvois did was to introduce some measure of order into the customary muddle of French military administration. The success or failure of armies depends in the last resort on the efficient organization of the supply services. Louvois, who was nicknamed the "great victualler," fully appreciated this fact. He devoted every care to building up supply depots and dumps and to manufacturing and transporting munitions. In particular, he arranged that stocks should be accumulated during the winter so that the army could always begin an early campaigning season. In those days, when it was the normal and accepted usage for soldiers to lay down their arms from October until the late spring, and for officers to return to hearth and home during the winter, the army which could take the field again first gained a high degree of strategic surprise and was often able to dictate the course of the subsequent battle.

After providing for munitions and supplies, the next most essential need of a proficient army is adequate and regular pay. French regiments consisted almost entirely of volunteers, and only reasonably good conditions of service were likely to produce good soldiers. But the French army did not escape the abuses that were current in most seventeenth-century armies, because company and battalion commanders were personally responsible for the payment of the troops. These officers purchased their commissions as a financial investment and were concerned to make as large a profit out of paying their men as they could. The commonest way of profiting at the expense of the State was for captains to pretend that their companies contained more men than they really did; for this purpose additional men would be hired on the occasion of inspection or ceremonial parades. Such soldiers of straw were called "faggots." Louvois vainly tried to root out this abuse by imposing the severest penalties, but it continued.

The officer class, which thus filled its purses, was mainly recruited from the nobility—and it was the only profession or business that this privileged class was permitted to practise. Officer training was liable to be both haphazard and empirical; although for a time cadet companies were established, they had little success. Strict discipline was, however, the order of the day. One of the inspectors of the French infantry regiments gave the word "martinet" to the English language. The King's insistence upon discipline not only from the men but from the highest ranking officers in his armies is well attested; dire punishment awaited failures and recalcitrants.

Until the reign of Louis XIV most of the arms of the service except the cavalry had been neglected. The infantryman had as his weapon a clumsy musket. To use the musket the soldier had first to load it with ball and powder, then to set light to a fuse by striking tinder. After this, the musket was raised to the shoulder and aimed on a wooden fork stuck in the ground; finally it was fired by the lighted fuse moving the primer. About the middle of the century a flintlock, which greatly simplified the mechanism of firing, had been invented, but Louvois was extremely cautious in introducing it into the French army. In 1687 Vauban invented a socket by which a bayonet could be attached to the musket without interfering with its firing. By this means pikemen could be abolished and the effectiveness of the infantry doubled. Similarly, during the reign of Louis XIV grenadiers and mounted infantry were gradually introduced. Thus the cavalry, led by the famous blue-clad Household Troops and Gendarmerie, were given solid support by the less glamorous foot-sloggers.

At the same time the artillery and engineers began to come into their own largely through the exertions of Vauban, who made use of them in siege warfare, which became the principal feature of the many Flanders campaigns. In conducting a siege Vauban's method was first to surround the fortress which was being attacked with parallel lines of entrenchments and then to launch from them mortar bombs, the range of which was calculated with mathematical accuracy, upon the enemy forces. The whole plan of a siege, with the prescribed entrenchments, sapping, and mortaring, was usually worked out in such precise detail that the date of the final assault and capitulation could be exactly estimated in advance. Ladies would be invited as witnesses of the last stages of a siege, and the final assault would take place to the accompaniment of violins. Louis XIV loved a good siege—the bigger the better—and would graciously accept the credit for all Vauban's hard work. Vauban also invented equally effective measures for the defence of French towns and built a magnificent ring of fortresses to protect the national frontiers. It was rightly said that "a town besieged by Vauban was a town captured—a town defended by Vauban was impregnable."

The ways in which French armies were raised varied and sometimes were of questionable value. The press-gang method was severely criticized by Vauban, while an attempt that was made to revert to mediæval principles of recruiting as a feudal obligation was unsuccessful. The conditions of pay and service, however, attracted sufficient volunteers not only inside France but from neighbouring countries like Piedmont and Switzerland. By 1679 the French army consisted of nearly 280,000 men, a truly remarkable strength for a time when populations were very much smaller than they are today. Under able generals like Turenne and Villars the French army gave an excellent account of itself, and had it not been for the rather uninspired manner in which it was directed by the King and Louvois (who invariably exasperated the commanders in the field) its victories might have been even more striking than they were. Nevertheless, it was a powerful instrument, the mere existence of which largely explains the successes of French foreign policy during the first twenty years of Louis XIV's personal rule.

The Dutch, on the other hand, on whom Louis XIV was now to wage war, suffered from internal dissensions and inter-State jealousies and had only a small and badly distributed army. The leader of the Dutch, John de Witt, was an energetic and devoted patriot; but he suffered from handicaps: one was that he was only the First Minister of the province of Holland and had to concert plans for the defence of the whole United Netherlands by soliciting the support of the six other provinces, which were always jealous of the supremacy of Amsterdam. Secondly, he was tarred with the brush of his former pro-French foreign policy. As late as 1666 de Witt had shown how deferential he was to French opinion by ordering the pro-English tutors and servants of the youthful Prince William of Orange, whose principal guardian he was, to leave the country. At this date William was only sixteen years old. Events proved that it was he and not his guardian who was to inspire the Dutch people in their resistance to Louis XIV.

William came of a remarkable family. His great-grandfather, William the Silent, although born a Roman Catholic and brought up as a protégé of Spain, had won the independence of the United Netherlands at the price of a long and bitter war against the Spanish monarchy. Thenceforward it became the rule that the Captain-General and Stadtholder (a kind of State presidency) of the important provinces of Holland and Zeeland should always be a prince of the House of Orange. In 1654, in consequence of a secret treaty between de Witt and Oliver Cromwell, it was agreed that William should be excluded from these offices in Holland. In 1667 a Perpetual Edict was passed by the State of Holland providing that the two offices might not be held by the same man. Such were the inauspicious conditions of William's upbringing. He was a pale youth with an aquiline nose who contracted asthma at the age of twelve. He enjoyed a good education and appears to have acquired many of the arts of statesmanship at an early age, his sensitive soul learning to steel itself against the polite insults heaped upon him by the Dutch republican oligarchy. The English ambassador at The Hague who met him in 1668 said that he "loved hunting as much as he hates swearing," that he preferred ale to wine, and was always sleepy by ten o'clock, and added that he was sensible and hard working. Such was the man who was the lifelong opponent of Louis XIV.

The army of the Dutch Union, of which William of Orange was made Captain-General in February 1672, contained some 55,000 men; but of these 34,000 were engaged on garrison duties, 9,000 were located in the Spanish Netherlands, and only 12,000 were available as a field army. When relations with France became tense, a large force was sent to garrison the town of Maastricht which, in view of its strategic position on the river Meuse, it was considered the French would have to attack before they could invade the United Provinces. In general the morale of the Dutch troops was not high and it was difficult for the Dutch Government to maintain a large field army because in time of danger the individual States had the habit of ordering their own contingents to return home.

In 1671 Louis XIV had completed his preparations for attacking the Dutch and had given his vast army some useful operational experience by invading Lorraine and occupying the country with French garrisons; by this means he cleared his flank and severed communications between the Dutch territories and the Spanish possessions of Netherland Provinces and Franche-Comté. In January 1672 the French King complained to the Dutch ambassador that his Government was "debauching my allies and trying to persuade my royal cousins to enter into offensive alliances against me." The real object of the war, however, was admitted to be that the annihilation of the Dutch was essential before the French monarchy could conquer the coveted Spanish Netherlands (modern Belgium). In May 1672 Louis XIV reviewed an army of over 100,000 men at Charleroi; probably so large an army had never been seen before in the western world. The French King ordered it forward against the Dutch without a declaration of war.

The methods by which Louis XIV prepared for this war, terrifying his neighbours into signing treaties of neutrality or assistance, building an enormous and well-equipped army, and finally striking at his chosen victim without warning, are the classical methods by which aggressive Great Powers are wont to act. These methods always give them an initial advantage and depend for their success upon the inability of their selected victim to hold out until the inevitable coalition which the aggressive Power provokes against itself has had time to form. On this occasion it was touch-and-go with the Dutch Republic. Prince Condé, who had based his army on Sedan, joined Turenne near Maastricht, and the wise military decision was taken to mask this fortress, and the main forces of France moved from the Meuse to the Rhine.

The Dutch made ready to man the line of the Ijssel, which runs southward from the Zuider Zee to join the river Leck near Arnheim. To reach the heart of Holland itself the French had either to penetrate this river barrier and enter the land of the dykes or launch an amphibious operation from the sea. On June 7 the Dutch admiral de Ruyter won an important victory over the English and French fleets at Southwold Bay, thus excluding the second alternative. At the same date, however, the French land forces succeeded in clearing the left bank of the Rhine and on June 12 crossed the river against only slight Dutch opposition. Turenne then seized Arnheim and thus outflanked the line of the Ijssel. The Dutch army withdrew to Utrecht, but this town was compelled to surrender by the end of the month. Amsterdam appeared defenceless. Condé wanted to push forward 6,000 cavalry to seize the town. Turenne, on this one vital occasion, was more prudent than his colleague and was backed in his opinion by the King and Louvois. The Dutch were thus given a respite in which to pierce the walls and dykes along the water-courses and to fill the "polders" or dry patches in this area between the rivers and canals. (They did not, as has sometimes been implied, flood the whole of Holland with the waters of the Zuider Zee.) In between the flooded districts the Dutch forces, amounting to only about nine thousand men, were stationed by William of Orange with orders to defend the main roads and waterways into Holland. Small naval craft armed with guns and manned by crews of thirty to forty men also guarded the water routes.

Meanwhile the Dutch sought peace and offered to surrender to the French Maastricht and various garrison towns (known as the Generality), the possession of which by the French would have enabled them to attack the Spanish Netherlands from the rear. Louis XIV, swayed, as he later confessed, by the notions of ambition and glory, "always pardonable in a prince," opened his mouth widely, asking for heavy compensation for his allies, a large indemnity, and substantial commercial and religious concessions. The Dutch refused to accept such humiliating terms. On July 8 William was elected Stadtholder under pressure of public opinion. On August 20 John de Witt and his brother were murdered at The Hague because they were held responsible for the war. The Elector of Brandenburg, the unique Dutch ally, appeared on the Lower Rhine with other German troops provided by the Emperor, and the French were compelled to divert a considerable force to meet this threat. The Dutch defence line held and by December William was able to sally forth to try to cut the French communications by attacking Charleroi. This bold manœuvre, although unsuccessful, gave the French a severe shock. Louis, together with the historians whom he had detailed to record his expected easy march to The Hague, had meanwhile retired to Saint-Germain for the winter. Unfortunately for himself, he had withdrawn too late. In the opinion of Sidney Godolphin, the future First Minister of Queen Anne, who had accompanied the French army in the role of an Allied observer, if the French King had gone back home earlier and had left Condé to direct operations the French army would have been in Amsterdam that summer. This campaign is therefore a good instance of the dangers of a divided command, for Louis was no general and Louvois, his War Minister, who accompanied him, constantly interfered with the commanders. The general in the field must be left to handle his own battle.

The campaign of 1673 opened auspiciously for France. Turenne advanced into Westphalia in the depth of winter and so harassed the forces of the Elector of Brandenburg that by the spring that egocentric prince was suing for peace. The French King permitted him to recover the territories that he had lost in return for a promise that he would stop helping the Dutch and acquiesce in the presence of French troops on German soil (Treaty of Vossem, April 10, 1673). Although the Dutch were thus deprived of their only effective ally, Louis XIV's plan of campaign for the summer season was uninspired. Turenne was left to guard the Rhine and the Moselle, Condé was put in command in Holland, where he impotently observed the rising floods and entertained himself by conversing with the Jewish philosopher, Spinoza, and Louis himself concentrated upon the siege of Maastricht. The King was accompanied on his progress to execute this feat of arms by his entire Court, complete with the Queen and the Marquise de Montespan, who was about to make him a father again. "Big sieges," the monarch announced, "please me more than others," and acting upon the dependable advice of Vauban, who was with him, he obtained the surrender of the city by July 1. A young English volunteer officer named John Churchill played a minor part in this success: a figure of ill omen for Louis's later career.

The King made the grave mistake of underrating his enemies. He spoke of the Dutch with scorn, while his chief adviser called them "beasts not men." The Dutch were unintimidated, and were, moreover, now united under William of Orange. They appreciated the value of sea power for the defence of their country. Admiral de Ruyter inflicted a further defeat on the French fleet off Zeeland (June 1673) and thereby prevented the army which was waiting in England, ready to assist Condé by a landing in the Dutch rear, from setting out. Thus cheered, the Dutch refused to consider the French peace terms which were put forward in a form almost unaltered from the far-reaching demands of 1672. The Dutch attitude was strengthened that summer by an accession of allies. The French King had roused the Spaniards by marching across Spanish territory to the siege of Maastricht. He had provoked the Emperor by operations in Germany. After difficult negotiations the Empire, Spain, and Lorraine concluded what was in effect an offensive alliance against France. In face of these threats Louis was obliged to withdraw Condé and some of his troops from Holland, thus enabling the Dutch leader to retake the important town of Naarden on September 7. On November 12 William of Orange was able to join his troops with the Imperial troops at Bonn in the territory of

France's ally, the Elector of Cologne. After pillaging Holland in a manner which even shocked Condé, the new French commander, Luxembourg, was compelled to carry out a withdrawal.

The "prodigious height of the waters" in Holland (in the words of Condé), the decisive victories of de Ruyter at sea, and the coalition which the French had raised against themselves, combined to ruin the original hopes of Louis XIV. He was now committed to a long war if he were to achieve the conclusive victory he wanted. The Dutch, on the other hand, thus saved from unimaginable perils, were determined to humble their mighty enemy, and William of Orange aspired not merely to punish the French King but to rob him of his gains in the earlier War of Devolution. France's allies began to desert her. Under pressure of Parliamentary opinion King Charles II of England was obliged to abandon his wealthy "brother" and concluded the Treaty of Westminster with the Dutch (February 1674), although some English regiments continued to serve under Turenne. The German princes abandoned their French paymaster, who in fact had often failed to pay them. By July 1674 the whole of Germany except Bavaria had turned against France, including the Hohenzollern Elector of Brandenburg, who changed sides once more. The only other remaining ally of France was Sweden, whose forces finally emerged from a state of military passivity to attack the Elector of Brandenburg and to suffer defeat at the battle of Fehrbellin (June 1675).

Nevertheless in 1674 the French army had helped to restore her King's tarnished prestige. Vauban took Besançon in Franche-Comté. Turenne successfully fought the Emperor's armies in Alsace, while Condé dealt with a combined Dutch and Spanish force in Flanders. On June 16 Turenne beat the Imperialists at the battle of Sinzheim near Heidelberg, and on August 11 Condé won the battle of Seneffe in Flanders after one of the most bloody struggles of the seventeenth century. Turenne, although faced by superior forces in Alsace and Lorraine, carried through a skilful winter campaign and once more won an important victory, this time at Turckheim (January 1675) and drove his enemies across the Rhine.

The French King's power was increased by these victories and also by dissensions among his opponents. He offered more moderate peace terms, found new allies in Hungary and Poland, and gained some successes in Flanders by taking Dinant, Huys, and Limburg before he returned to Versailles in July. But that month a grievous blow fell upon the French monarchy when Turenne, out on reconnaissance in Alsace, was killed by a stray shot. Condé, now become a cautious campaigner, took Turenne's place, and the Court of Versailles was instructed to console itself with the thought that although the greatest of French generals was dead, their King still lived. "Louis XIV did not, however, hurry to the menaced frontiers," comments M. Lavisse, "as he would have done had he possessed the soul of a soldier. Instead he wrote letters."

After the death of Turenne the French evacuated Alsace. Condé, who conducted the final stages of this withdrawal, subsequently retired from active service to engage in literary conversations and to attend to family affairs. The year 1676 was one of military stalemate. Louis XIV besieged the small towns of Bouchain and Aire in Flanders, whilst William of Orange unsuccessfully undertook a larger feat of arms at Maastricht. Both sides rigorously refused to engage the other in battle. On the Rhine the Imperialists took Philippsburg on September 17. In the Mediterranean the French fleet, now commanded by the Protestant and former pirate Duquesne, fought two battles with the Dutch in the first of which the celebrated de Ruyter was killed (April 22, 1676); these victories were followed by the French occupation of the town of Messina in Sicily, which then belonged to Spain.

In these inconclusive strategic circumstances it was natural that peace negotiations should be reopened. A congress was summoned at Nimweguen at the end of the year under the eager mediation of the English Government. Both sides were in the mood to offer concessions and difficulties arose less between the principals than between their allies. Louis XIV did not consider that it would become him to abandon the Swedes, his only faithful allies, while William of Orange did not want to leave France with any part of the Spanish Netherlands. A series of French victories in Flanders during 1677 tended to make the Dutch more accommodating. After the quick capture of Valenciennes (March 4) the King laid siege to Cambrai and his brother the Duke of Orleans attacked St. Omer. William of Orange, with a mixed Dutch and Spanish Army of 40,000 men, tried to prevent the fall of St. Omer but was severely defeated at the battle of Cassel (April 11), in which he lost 3,000 men and 4,000 prisoners. Louis, having done enough for glory, dispersed the French army to garrison duties and went back to Versailles. That winter, however, another French army under Créqui took its revenge for the loss of Philippsburg by crossing the Rhine after the Germans had taken up their winter quarters and captured Freiburg. The allies of France, Poland and Sweden, also achieved some successes. William of Orange could only retort with a triumph in the field of diplomacy; in November 1677 he married Mary, niece of the King of England—thus menacing Louis with an Anglo-Dutch coalition, which was a profound setback for his diplomacy since it meant the complete reversal of the policy of the Treaty of Dover.

Louis XIV now recognized that it was high time to make peace on the best terms that he could obtain. Messina was evacuated to gratify the two Maritime Powers. Then, after first showing the strength of his hand by launching a force of 120,000 men into Flanders in the spring of 1678 and capturing the important town of Ghent, the French King left his army and published his peace proposals. These terms were nicely calculated and would have been acceptable to the Dutch had the French King not insisted that before they were signed his faithful ally Sweden must have restored to her the territories taken by the Elector of Brandenburg. A definitive Anglo-Dutch alliance was concluded in July 1678 and a renewal of the war threatened if the French did not evacuate the towns which they had taken in Flanders without awaiting the settlement of the Swedish problem. However, an expedient was found: the Swedes promised to accept the peace settlement provided that the Dutch promised not to assist their ally, the Elector of Brandenburg.

By the Peace of Nimweguen (there was a group of treaties, including one signed between the French and Dutch on August 10, between France and Spain on September 17, and between France and the Emperor on February 26, 1679) the French gave up Maastricht and accepted reciprocal trading arrangements with the Dutch; although they restored Courtrai, Oudenarde, Ath, Charleroi (gained by the Treaty of Aix-la-Chapelle), Ghent, and Limburg (occupied during the war), they obtained from the Spaniards Franche Comté and a line of strong places running from Dunkirk to the Meuse, including St. Omer, Cassel, Ypres, Aire, Cambrai, Bouchain, Valenciennes, Condé, and Maubeuge. The Emperor agreed to exchange Freiburg for Philippsburg. The Duke of Lorraine was restored to his duchy, and in 1679 a French army was sent into the Rhenish provinces belonging to the Elector of Brandenburg to compel him to restore Western Pomerania to Sweden.

The Peace of Nimweguen represents the summit of Louis XIV's success. "I fully rejoice," he wrote in his *Memoirs*, "in my good luck and clever conduct whereby I was able to profit from every opportunity I found to extend the boundaries of my kingdom at the expense of my enemies." By his gains from Spain not only did he reaffirm the superiority of the Bourbons over the Habsburgs but he managed to strengthen the vulnerable northern, north-eastern, and south-eastern frontiers of his kingdom. His diplomacy, backed by the remarkable achievements of his large and efficient armies, which had never once been beaten during six years' campaign-

ing, had established beyond question the ascendancy of
France in Europe. Even his navy, after its early rebuffs
in the North Sea, had won respect by its victories in the
Mediterranean. He had made himself the arbiter of the
destinies of other States—notably of Sweden and Brandenburg.

It should be noticed that just as in 1666 Louis XIV
had been driven by considerations of personal prestige to
assist the Dutch against the English, so for much the
same reasons he had deliberately jeopardized his territorial gains in Flanders by insisting on fulfilling his
promises to Sweden. Here it can be said there was an
honourable and noble side to Louis XIV's policy of self-
glorification—it was against his nature to break his word,
if publicly given, to an ally. And honour paid a dividend,
for these precedents advertised the value of a French
alliance. But Louis's policy carried with it the seeds of
future misery for France. The Prussian rulers at Berlin
were never to forgive or forget the check which the
French army had imposed upon their expansionist ambitions. Moreover Louis XIV, by estranging not only
the Elector of Brandenburg but other German princes,
had thrown Austrians, Prussians, and Southern Germans
into a coalition against him. By abandoning the policy
of Richelieu and Mazarin he had united a resentful
Germany (as far as it was then capable of unity) against
him. Just over a century later Napoleon was by a similar
policy of deliberate aggression also to assist in the ultimate
unification of Germany. The French people had to learn
through many years of hard wars that in the long run a
policy of unprovoked aggression directed to territorial
expansion does not pay. Nor did this policy prove really
profitable even during Louis XIV's own reign. By refusing to offer the Dutch reasonable peace terms at a
time when they would have been compelled to accept
them Louis XIV not only created an implacable enemy
in the person of William of Orange but helped to fashion an Anglo-Dutch alliance based upon the support
of much informed public opinion in both countries even

though the two nations were rivals in matters of commerce. French diplomacy was able to disrupt this alliance temporarily when Charles II and James II sat on the English throne; but in the end it was this combination of virile Protestant Powers which defeated the French King's plan for his descendants to take over the whole empire of the decadent Spanish Habsburgs.

Chapter 6

Church and King

SOON AFTER THE signature of the Treaty of Nimweguen a striking change took place in the character of the French King: Louis, who had not merely tasted but feasted upon the pleasures of love, war, and power, turned his attention towards religion: he became a "dévot."

"The King," wrote Mme de Maintenon in April 1679, "is full of excellent sentiments and often reads the Holy Scriptures which he finds the finest of all books. He confesses his weaknesses and recognizes his faults. We must now wait for the spirit of Grace to disclose itself. He is thinking seriously about the conversion of heretics and in a little while he will work on this subject to some purpose." The King was over forty, and hitherto he had taken his religion for granted in childlike innocence. He was now prepared actively to renounce his life of sensuous pleasure. About to marry the intelligent, pious, and middle-aged Mme de Maintenon, he was willing to spend time and energy on the internal as well as the external affairs of his kingdom. And the problem which appeared to him to be in most urgent need of solution was that of the relations between Church and State.

It has sometimes been said that it was in fact the influence of Mme de Maintenon herself which attracted his thoughts in this direction. It is true that her influence was not negligible and that he often invited her opinions. But she represented less a decisive influence than a phase in his spiritual and intellectual development. Mlle de La Vallière, Mme de Montespan, and Mme de Maintenon have well been described as symbolizing the spring, midsummer, and autumn of Louis XIV's life. Moreover, in this gradual transition from an attitude of careless gaiety to one of religious devotion he was merely following a psy-

chological trend which might be detected in the careers
of his most distinguished subjects. For example, the cynical La Fontaine, the dramatist Racine, and the beautiful
Louise de La Vallière all passed their later years in an
atmosphere of conspicuous piety. The monasteries and
convents not infrequently welcomed lovely women whose
bloom was fading and once brilliant courtiers who had
drunk the cup of life to the full to meditate upon the
eternal and prepare for the adventure of death. It had, for
example, been with the utmost reluctance that Marshal
Turenne had under pressure retained his command in
France's hour of need instead of retiring to a life of religious devotion so that he could in the end confront with
a quiet mind the Maker in whom he believed.

But this trend of religious feeling in the King merely
served to reinforce the political convictions which he had
long held strongly. Believing, as he did, that he was monarch by direct choice of the Deity and that his powers were
bestowed from on high, he felt a personal sense of
responsibility for the religious life of all his subjects. He
even saw himself, somewhat as Henry VIII of England
had done, as supreme head of the Church as well as of
the State, and considered that it was clearly incompatible
with the grandeur and unity of his realm for there to be
any symptoms of heresy or schism anywhere in the land.
And yet when he looked around the signs were only too
plain. At the prime of his life Louis was stirred to set this
wrong aright.

The Church of France or the Gallican Church was,
however, only a part of the universal Roman Catholic
Church and as such it acknowledged with certain limitations the authority of the Pope. The King recognized but
in his early days resented this, for it qualified his ability
to carry out reforms. To unify the French Church by
eliminating all dissentient or discordant elements required
not merely the approval but the active assistance of the
Bishop of Rome, "a foreign Power," for the papacy at that
time ruled a sizable independent State. Consequently the
history of Church and State during Louis XIV's reign

comprised two aspects: first was the King's intention, inspired both by a desire to reinforce the unity of his kingdom and by genuine, if crude, notions of crusading zeal, to impose religious conformity on all his subjects; secondly, there was the anxiety of the monarchy to avoid recognizing the claim of the Popes as heads of the Catholic Church to interfere with the internal administration of the French Church. (This anxiety was enhanced by the knowledge that the papacy had on the whole favoured the Spanish Habsburgs, rather than the French Bourbons, in mundane affairs.)

In both these policies the King had the backing of the majority of the French clergy, for the tradition of an independent and unified Church was an old and understandable one. But these two policies were in conflict. For not only did the suppression of heresy and schism demand the support and approval of the Pope, but the independence of the French Church was contrary to its nature as a branch of the Church Universal. How could the French Church persecute Protestants and at the same time demand in large measure the rights of the Protestant Churches? How could the King require heretics to renounce their heresies as being contradictory to the teachings of the Catholic Church, if at the same time he was casting doubt upon the claims of the Pope to define Catholic doctrine—for if the Pope did not interpret Church doctrine, then who did? All these difficulties were of course susceptible of solution by the French theologians. Nevertheless, if these questions were regarded not as philosophical problems but as straightforward political issues, they were not easy to resolve. In practice the French ruler was obliged in the end to acquiesce in most of the claims of the papacy, for the simple reason that he regarded the word "schism as too horrible to repeat"— he did not wish to follow the example of Henry VIII. On the other hand, the Popes had no intention of forcing the French Church to break away, thereby losing the allegiance of the richest and most powerful kingdom in the world. Hence to a large extent this revival of the historic struggle between Church and State was unreal, because neither side wished to drive the other to extremities.

At the beginning of Louis XIV's period of personal rule there was a variety of quarrels between the French Government and Rome. The King's ministers were indeed more anti-papist than the King. Colbert was, as has been stated, an anti-clerical at heart because he not only considered that the French monks were useless citizens in themselves but because he held that they encouraged idleness in others by their charitable provision for the needy and out-of-work. Lionne, the King's first Foreign Minister, was an opponent of the papacy because he considered that the claim of the Pope to interfere in the internal affairs of France could not be reconciled with a vigorous nationalist foreign policy. The humiliation of the papacy over the affair of the Corsican guards in 1662 augured well for the Gallican party; but this was a victory on a purely political plane. When in 1666 the Pope complained about Colbert's policy towards the religious houses, the King gave way. He also acquiesced in the promulgation of a papal bull condemning the Faculty of Theology for censuring writings at the Sorbonne which upheld the doctrine of papal infallibility.

The main conflict of the reign came over the question of the "régale." The word "régale" meant the royal prerogative to exercise the temporal and spiritual rights pertaining to the diocese of a bishop from the time that the incumbent died until his successor was instituted. The assertion of this right by a royal declaration which had retrospective force brought protests from two bishops and they were supported in their objections by Pope Innocent XI (elected in 1676), a man of austere behaviour, humble manners, and a crusading spirit who (in the words of Mme de Sévigné) did not tremble but threatened. The French clergy, although they disliked the right of régale, were for the most part deferential to the monarchy and resented the Pope's interference. An assembly, which met in 1681 under the leadership of Bossuet, Bishop of Meaux, propounded four articles defining what it regarded as the true position of the Church in relation to the papacy.

The first article reaffirmed the sovereign's independence of the spiritual power in secular matters; the second appeared to assert the superiority of Councils of the Church over the Pope; the third insisted upon the traditional limitations imposed by the constitution of the French Church upon papal acts within the French kingdom; and the fourth stated somewhat obscurely that "even in questions of faith the decision of the Pope is not incapable of amendment, so long as it is without the approval of the Church." In sum these articles maintained that the papacy had no right to overrule the King on temporal matters, such as in his presentations to benefices, while the French clergy were excepted from the doctrinal authority of the Roman Court. "It was the opinion of contemporaries," wrote Ranke, "that although France might remain within the pale of the Catholic Church, it yet stood on the threshold in readiness for stepping beyond it."

Innocent XI took up this challenge by refusing to institute those clergy of secondary rank who had taken part in the meeting of the assembly and were subsequently promoted to bishoprics by a grateful king. And the King for his part refused to ask for the institution of bishops who had not attended the assembly. In 1688 thirty-five dioceses had no bishop. For some time both Pope and King adopted an adamant attitude; the King gave orders that the doctrines embodied in the four Gallican articles should be taught universally, and the Pope announced that he would rather die than abandon his rights. However, a compromise was eventually reached. The French bishops were persuaded in 1693 to write a letter withdrawing anything in the articles which could be construed as incompatible with the papal prerogatives and expressing "unspeakable grief" for what they had done. But this letter was never published, nor were the articles ever officially withdrawn.

Later, further disputes between Louis XIV and the Pope followed. In 1687 there was a quarrel over the behaviour of the French ambassador in Rome, whose threatening conduct and insistence on the extra-territorial rights of his embassy caused Innocent to excommunicate him. Louis replied by appealing to a General Council and by seizing the papal estate of Avignon. A reconciliation took place after the death of Innocent in 1689, when the King restored Avignon and entered into negotiations.

That there was a certain amount of play-acting about all these quarrels is clear from the fact that in the end a compromise was always reached. But it is also shown by a curious incident. In February 1682, just at the time when the public dispute over the régale had reached its climax, Louis XIV begged the Pope to approve the installation of his ten-year-old illegitimate son by Mme de Montespan in certain abbey properties that were intended for his sustenance. The Pope duly granted the royal prayer on behalf of the chubby abbot-elect and the King graciously accepted this singular mark of "paternal affection" towards him. "We must not look at historical personages only when they are in the public eye," wrote M. Lavisse sagely of this episode. "In public they strike attitudes; they discuss business in the corridors."

One reason why the King was moderate in his dealings with the papacy was that he found he needed to invoke the help of the head of the Catholic Church in disciplining an important section of the French Church whom he regarded as heretics, namely the Jansenists. The Jansenists were named after a Flemish bishop who had written two books on the teaching of St. Augustine. Broadly the Jansenists taught a doctrine, akin to that of the Calvinists, that Christians could be saved only if they were predestined to eternal happiness in the after-life by being in receipt of grace from on high; without such grace, the Jansenists maintained, neither devotions nor confessions would help Christians, although even if a believer had grace, salvation was by no means assured. Like the Puritan Calvinists, the Jansenists were men and women of severe morals who regarded most popular forms of pleasure—such as dancing —as sinful. One Jansenist bishop refused absolution to

army officers who had taken up winter quarters in his
diocese on the ground that they would have done better
to have left the King's service rather than "to live at the
people's expense." Holding such views, the Jansenists
naturally looked upon the private life and habits of the
French King with jaundiced eyes, and supported the well-
founded complaints of the Marquis de Montespan about
the behaviour of his wife. The King on his side came to
regard the Jansenists not only as heretics but also as very
likely republicans.

Louis XIV's antipathy towards the Jansenists was animated and reinforced by his Jesuit confessors, Père La
Chaise and Père Le Tellier. The Jesuits taught a very
different doctrine of salvation from that of the Jansenists,
allowing, as they did, that a generous scale of expiable sins
did not bar the road to Heaven. Moreover, the Jesuits
were internationalists and were the supporters of the highest claims of the Pope. The Jansenists, on the other hand,
invoked the independence of the French Church with its
tradition of resisting papal encroachments, to protect
themselves against condemnation by Rome for heresy.
(The matter is a little complicated by the fact that, partly
for tactical reasons, the Jansenists had sided with the
Pope against the King over the question of the régale.)
To counterbalance the Jansenists' claim to interpret doctrine with rigid reference to efficient grace the King was
virtually driven to invoke papal infallibility. The paradoxi-
cal result of the King's series of attacks on the Jansenists
was therefore that they ended against the wishes of many
of his advisers and his most influential subjects in his sac-
rificing the monarchy's proud independence of the papacy.

When Louis first took over the reins of government the
Jansenist movement was not very strong. Five propositions extracted (as the Jesuits claimed) from Jansen's
Augustinus had already been condemned as heretical by
the Pope in 1653. The Jansenists were ordered to sign a
formula in which they disavowed these propositions. They
said that they agreed that the propositions denounced by
the Jesuits were heretical, but denied that they could be

found in the books of Jansen. The two main centres of Jansenist influence were two nunneries, one the Port-Royal in Paris, the other the Port-Royal des Champs near Versailles; near the latter there was also a male community which included the great essayist Blaise Pascal. In 1661 Mother Angélique, the head of Port-Royal des Champs, died, and within the next two years Pascal and his sister, Sainte-Euphémie, also died. Only four of the bishops were Jansenists. Neither the Jansenist clergy nor the nuns would sign the papal formula, and in 1665 Louis XIV demanded the help of Pope Clement IX for the enforcement of discipline against them. The Pope sent a nuncio named Bargellini to Paris who organized a clever compromise, in agreement with the French Foreign Minister, Lionne, whereby the Jansenists were merely asked to accept a formula renouncing the five propositions "sincerely" but not "purely and simply"—in other words, they were not compelled to admit that heretical doctrines were to be found in Jansen's book.

The Bargellini compromise, however, failed to destroy the Jansenist movement, which received the eager protection and encouragement of such former Frondeur leaders as Cardinal Retz and the King's cousin, Mme de Longueville. The accession of Innocent XI strengthened the position of the Jansenists, since the new Pope was grateful for their support over the question of the régale while he disliked some of the "laxist" teachings of the Jesuits. Consequently the King's demand that he should be allowed to nominate the abbesses of the Port-Royal convents was refused. The Jansenists acquired another influential protector when in 1695 Noailles, Bishop of Chalons, was nominated Archbishop of Paris. A prolonged and complicated struggle continued until the end of the reign. On one side were ranged the King—who thrust forty or fifty Jansenists into the Bastille—his Jesuit advisers, and the versatile Archbishop Fénelon; on the other were the new Archbishop of Paris, the celebrated bishop Bossuet, and the dramatist Racine. The Jesuits gained a notable victory when in June 1703 an agreement was signed between the

King and Pope Clement XI to suppress the Jansenists, and another when in 1710 Louis XIV succeeded in effecting the dissolution of the Port-Royal convents and in enjoying the somewhat petty satisfaction of seeing the remains of eminent Jansenists pulled from the grave and thrown to the dogs. The Jansenists, for their part, enlisted the majority of the French clergy and the lawyers of the Parliament of Paris on their side. They modified and spread their doctrines widely, making many converts. Two papal bulls condemning Jansenist doctrines, although welcomed by the King, were ignored by the French clergy, who regarded them as a violation of Gallican privileges and as exemplifying unadmitted claims to papal infallibility.

In his last years the old King was torn between two sets of advisers—those who exalted the independence of the French Church and told him that constantly to invoke the help of the Pope was to undermine his own power, and those who taught that he must closely ally himself with the papacy in order to extirpate heresy and republicanism from France. On the whole, thinking of his latter end, he inclined "not to anger the Pope." What would have happened had Louis XIV lived longer and brought the question to a final issue with his civilian and ecclesiastical counsellors is hard to say. But in his unrelenting opposition to Port-Royal the King was undoubtedly right from his own point of view. The Jansenists, with their high moral ideals and aims, were logically enemies of a régime which was governed by ideas of autocracy and nationalist grandeur. A connexion may be traced between the Jansenist movement which Louis XIV vainly tried to suppress and the anti-clerical revolutionaries who destroyed the ancient monarchy.

The Jansenists at least claimed to be Catholics and therefore some argument might take place about whether they were or were not heretical. There could, however, be no doubt about the status of the French Protestants, whose privileges were considered by almost all Roman Catholics to be an excrescence on the unity of the realm which boasted as its ruler the Most Christian King. These privileges had been granted to the Huguenots (as the French Protestants were called) by Louis XIV's grandfather, Henry IV, himself a Protestant before he had allowed himself to be converted in order to obtain the throne. The Edict of Nantes, promulgated by Henry IV in 1598, while stating that Catholicism was the established religion of France, allowed Protestants to worship freely in those places where their religion had been established in 1597. Protestants were permitted by this Edict to hold all offices open to other citizens and special tribunals were set up to protect their interests. Since the time when this Edict became law the Huguenots had been exemplary subjects and in particular had refrained from trying to improve their position by taking part in the wars of the Fronde. They served loyally in the French army and navy, and produced one of the greatest French generals in Turenne, whose protection they lost, however, on his conversion in 1668.

In 1661 there were some million Huguenots in France, mainly concentrated in the provinces of Normandy, Poitou, and Languedoc. Excluded in fact, if not by law, from the most important offices of State, they had made remarkable headway not only in industry and commerce (where, like the Jews, they had provoked the jealousy of their less successful competitors) but also in the professions, especially medicine. Most influential Roman Catholic citizens tended, therefore, to envy the industrious Huguenots; many also regarded them not only as unpatriotic but as a dangerous influence in a Catholic kingdom. Surely, it was said, there should be no serious difficulty in converting these heretics? Was not the Edict of Nantes, after all, a temporary political expedient not intended to prevent the people of the good land of France from becoming united again in one universal faith?

In the early years of his reign Louis XIV, who was not yet a "dévot," appears to have acquiesced in the policy represented by the Edict of Nantes. The Assembly of the Clergy, however, constantly pressed the monarch to do something for God who had done so much for him; and what service could be more acceptable than the suppression of heresy? Although it granted him large sums of money by way of a sweetener, the King expressed his intention of abiding by the policy of the Edict. The Edict had nevertheless already been undermined. Many Protestant churches or "temples," as they were called, were destroyed on the ground that they had been built since 1598. Limitations were imposed on the subjects that might be taught in the Protestant schools. Bossuet, assisted among others by the Jansenists, had embarked on an ambitious conversion campaign. And an office was opened which offered converts the modest sum of six livres for signing on the dotted line.

Such was the situation when the Treaty of Nimweguen left the King free to contemplate the need for internal reforms in his kingdom. Many factors caused him to change his outlook. In the first place he was anxious to show the world that he was a good Catholic. He might have had his differences with the Pope, but he was a loyal son of the Church. He might have taken part in a double adultery with Mme de Montespan, but now he was about to become the faithful husband of the religious Mme de Maintenon. The whole atmosphere of the Court was gradually changed, and the gay fêtes of the early Versailles yielded before the scenes of model domesticity at Saint-Cyr. The King set a public example of devoutness. "The King is beginning to think seriously of his salvation," wrote Mme de Maintenon in 1681; "if God preserves his life, there will soon by only one religion in his kingdom."

Secondly, there were powerful political reasons why Louis XIV should dislike the Protestants. "The Huguenots were painted to him in black colours," wrote Saint-Simon. "They were described as a State within a State, brought to this point of licence in consequence of disorders, revolts, civil wars, alliances with foreign countries, and open resistance to the kings who were his predecessors." And so the new "dévot" was moved by the happy thought that he could buy an easy penance at the expense of others, a penance which would see him straight into a world of bliss. Although Mme de Maintenon unquestionably approved his decision to destroy heretics, it does not seem that her influence was dominant. The main instrument of this reactionary policy was the War Minister, Louvois, who after 1684 had no war on his hands and fancied himself as proselyte in chief. The sycophantic Colbert, who in earlier times had done much to protect the industrious Huguenots and confound the Jesuits, scented which way the wind blew and acquiesced.

During the years 1680 to 1684 a wholesale offensive was made on the Protestants and no method was left unexplored which would convert the Edict of Nantes into a dead letter. Offices and professions were forbidden to the Huguenots. The special tribunals established under the Edict were suppressed in 1679. Conversions or reconversions to Protestantism were severely punished. Schools were attacked; mixed marriages were prohibited. Local attacks upon Protestant churches were intensified and in two dioceses the delighted bishops by one chicanery or another managed to have every "temple" demolished. It was said that by 1685 570 out of 815 Protestant places of worship had been closed.

While these repressive measures were pursued in every direction, positive steps were taken to win converts. It was announced that every Protestant child over seven years of age might opt for the Catholic Church and then be abducted from his parents' care. Births and deaths of Protestants were placed as far as possible in Catholic control; for only Catholic midwives might function, and they were ordered to register all children whose survival was uncertain as baptized Catholics; at the other end of the human scale doctors attending the Protestant sick and dying were expected to notify Catholic priests so that souls might be snatched en route to the beyond.

The most powerful instrument of conversion was the "dragonnades." It had long been customary for the French army to billet soldiers on civilians, but French dragoons were now deliberately billeted on the richest and most influential Huguenot households with orders to make themselves as unpleasant as they could be. In some provinces torture was employed to gain converts. Protest meetings against these excesses were ignored. Converts were rewarded with exemption from taxation and billeting. In Poitou, where the policy of the dragonnades was enforced most ruthlessly, thirty thousand converts were made a year.

The decision to revoke the Edict of Nantes was taken by Louis in 1685 on the ground that it had now become superfluous. The wonderful series of conversions in the preceding five years had, it was argued, reduced the Huguenots to an insignificant minority. The entire Court approved this drastic step. Louvois was delighted; Colbert was dead; Le Tellier was dying. The King's wife and confessor approved of his decision as the act of an apostle. "It is a work worthy of your reign," said the gifted Bossuet. "Through you heresy is no more; God alone has performed this miracle."

The revocation of the Edict, signed by the King on October 18, ordered the demolition of all Protestant temples, the cessation of all Protestant services, the closure of all Protestant schools, the Catholic baptism of those born in the Protestant faith. The revocation was enforced with the greatest brutality. The dragonnades were renewed and extended under the direction of their most experienced professors. Men were tortured, women stripped naked and whipped. Thousands of Protestants attempting to flee the country were sent to the galleys. Ministers caught trying to hold services were put to death.

In spite of all these efforts heresy was not extirpated from the State. As in later days and in other countries a persecuted minority, helped by friends at home and sympathizers abroad, managed to escape across the national frontiers. Many crossed the Alps, others found boats to take them from southern ports. It is estimated that about 200,000 persons left France and settled abroad. Sixty thousand made their way to England, where they established a silk industry in London and a tapestry manufacture in Exeter. Others found a welcome in Holland and

Brandenburg. The King regarded the exodus as a nuisance
rather than as an evil, and was more concerned at the
treatment of those who remained behind. It was obvious
that the enforced conversions were not likely to be dura-
ble, and there were not enough qualified Catholic priests
or teachers to bring up this generation of new converts.
In 1698 a royal declaration commended the new converts
to the particular care of the Catholic hierarchy. Nevertheless persecution continued and so did the secret exercise
of the Protestant religion. The resentful minorities which
remained, notably in the mountains of the Cevennes, were
to be a running sore to the French kingdom in the later
years of Louis XIV's reign.

Saint-Simon thus sums up (although with some rhetorical exaggeration) the consequences of the revocation of
the Edict of Nantes:

> The revocation of the Edict of Nantes, decided upon
> without the least excuse or any need, and the many
> proscriptions as well as declarations that followed it
> constituted a terrible plot which depopulated one-quar-
> ter of the kingdom, destroyed its commerce, enfeebled
> all parties, caused widespread pillage and condoned the
> dragonnades, allowed tortures and torments in which
> many innocent persons of both sexes died by thousands,
> ruined a numerous people, tore families to pieces, set
> relatives against one another in a fight for food and
> property, caused our manufacturers to move abroad,
> where they flourished and brought wealth to other
> States at our expense and enabled new and flourishing
> towns to be built, and gave them the spectacle of so re-
> markable a people being proscribed, stripped of their
> possessions, exiled, made to wander over the face of
> the earth without being guilty of any crime, seeking
> shelter from their own country.

Louis XIV, it has been said, by revoking the Edict of
Nantes was only behaving in a manner natural to his age
and century. Had not English Catholics been persecuted

by Cromwell? Had not the "Popish Plot" of Charles II's reign been little more than a Protestant orgy? These were weighty, although not indisputable, arguments: for men like Descartes and Bayle had already begun to preach toleration and the Dutch were starting to practise it. But whatever the reasons or excuses for the policy of intolerance may have been—and perhaps they were not, judged by one standard, ignoble—the immediate results and the long-term consequences were alike serious for France. The French King's methods of dealing with religious problems were unsuccessful in all their aspects. The policy adopted towards the Huguenots, like that employed towards the Jansenists and the papacy, ended (as M. Lavisse wrote) in political and moral bankruptcy.

Chapter 7

The Prime of Life

LOUIS, WHO IN his forties had successfully challenged the combined might of Europe, had imposed a pattern of unity upon his kingdom by suppressing Protestantism, and had settled his own domestic affairs, was a very different man from the somewhat diffident young prince who had taken over supreme power from his foster-father twenty years before; he was sure of his statecraft and sure of himself. He knew, or thought he knew, all the secrets of life and of the Court which epitomized his life, but he guarded the secrets of government jealousy even from his own ministers. He was never bored or tired; he always showed the same calm and majestic exterior to the world. "No fatigue, no accident of the weather mortified him or made any impression on that air of grandeur or that heroic figure; pierced by rain, snow, cold, or sweat or covered with dust, he was always the same," He could charm by his voice and by the way he handled those with whom he dealt. He was usually simply dressed, wearing no jewels except for the diamond buckles on his shoes. Physically time had wrought its changes: he had lost all his teeth, his jaw had dropped, and the marks of smallpox showed more plainly, but his grave and even morose face suited the nature of his responsible duties from which he rarely or never relaxed. There was now a suspicion of *embonpoint*. His sister-in-law, the German second wife of the King's brother, Philip of Orleans, wrote:

It cannot be denied that Louis XIV was the finest man in his kingdom; nobody had a better presence than he; his figure was agreeable, his legs well made, his feet small, his voice pleasant; he was lusty in propor-

tion; and in short, no fault could be found with his
person. Some people thought he was too corpulent
for his height, and that Monsieur (his brother) was
too short; so that it was said by way of a joke at Court,
that there had been a mistake, and that one brother had
received what had been intended for the other. The
King was in the habit of keeping his mouth open in an
awkward way.

As he advanced deeper into middle age the King suffered from a variety of small illnesses, but even as physical
grace left him, there remained the undeniable and sustained air of majesty. Though his manners were easy and
confident, he had to pay a price for supreme responsibility. Gone was the rapture of those idyllic youthful days
when he romanced with Marie Mancini or played the
guitar in his bathroom. "If he knew the art of reigning,"
wrote the Duchess of Burgundy, "he was never a moment
without exercising it; and therefore he was never at ease
with anyone, nor was anyone at ease with him—not even
his mistresses." At this stage in life his habits and manners
were fixed. Those soliciting favours could obtain an
audience with him at Court five or six times a day and
would be heard patiently and politely before they received
the invariable answer, "I will see," for nothing could be
settled lightly.

Louis never said anything calculated to give pain and
he reprimanded his servants but rarely. Yet he insisted
on his authority. Even to the routine requests put forward
by his ministers he would give an occasional refusal "to
show that he was the master and would not be governed."
For Louis was proud and jealous. Although he loved his
bejewelled and rather effeminate brother, he refused ever
to give him another command after he had been in
nominal charge at the victorious battle of Cassel in 1677,
for that would have been to throw a screen across the light
of the sun. Lionne's successor, Pomponne, was dismissed,
possibly because he was of a Jansenist family, in November 1679; Colbert died in September 1684, universally

execrated because of the heavy taxes which he had imposed; and the invaluable, if sinister, Louvois died in 1691. The King would not admit that these losses made any difference to the efficiency of his government. He merely redoubled his own labours. Mme de Maintenon wrote that his closest acquaintances were astonished by his activity at this period: "From six to ten at night he never ceased to read, write, or dictate, and after supper he soon dismissed the princesses to speed some courier on his journey."

The King's chief relaxation at this time in his life was hunting, to which he invariably devoted two or three hours a day. His other pleasures included billiards, watching comedies at Saint-Cyr, and eating. "I have often seen the King eat four platefuls of different soups," records his sister-in-law, "a whole pheasant, a partridge, a plateful of salad, mutton hashed with garlic, two good-sized slices of ham, a dish of pastry, and afterwards fruit and sweetmeats." Although a big eater, according to Saint-Simon, he was not a greedy one, for he knew his own capacity, while he was a most modest drinker, always mixing water with wine. In general the King's pleasures at this stage in his life were limited and innocent; the extravagances of his youth lay behind him. This change may be partly attributed to his wife, Mme de Maintenon.

"The Court of France," wrote the Duchess of Orleans, "was extremely agreeable until the King had the misfortune to marry that old Maintenon; she withdrew him from company, filled him with ridiculous scruples concerning plays, and told him that he ought not to see excommunicated persons."

Life at Court was still impressive to the visitor—the King entering his carriage, accompanied by his cohorts of guards, servants, and courtiers, reminded an Italian of a queen bee taking to the fields with her swarm—but the vitality and gaiety of the early Versailles had vanished. The King now excluded everyone who smacked of the libertine or smelt of the Jansenist, and thought that everyone who did not profess the faith of the Jesuits was irretrievably damned. During Easter 1684 comedy was banned from Versailles and opera from Paris, and talking at Mass was forbidden. A puritan wind began to sweep the once joyous corridors of the royal palaces, but the courtiers still worshipped the King, and the King worshipped God. The courtiers did as etiquette demanded, danced to the measured music chosen by their monarch, and tried to redeem their ruined fortunes at the gaming tables. "There is a certain order of things that never changes," wrote a lady of the Court, "always the same pleasures, always at the same time, and always with the same people." The Court balls, wrote the same lady, which began about midnight and ended punctually at two, were dreary affairs; and no entertainments were allowed to interfere with the attention that was due to war. And war, or its equivalent, was perpetual.

Louis XIV was determined to press home the advantages which he had acquired by the Peace of Nimweguen, if not by waging war then by the threat of war against his weakened neighbours. He felt inspired to earn more fully the title of Louis the Great which had been conferred upon him in 1680 by the city of Paris. His first step was to appoint a new Foreign Minister. The reason given out publicly for the dismissal of Pomponne was that he had delayed showing him an important dispatch. Pomponne was replaced by Colbert de Croissi (the younger brother of Jean-Baptiste Colbert) who had been ambassador to London and a plenipotentiary at Nimweguen. It was possibly from Colbert de Croissi that Louis XIV took the idea of extending the French empire by legal ingenuity, backed by the threat of force. But since the procedure adopted was not dissimilar from that employed when the French King invoked the so-called Law of Devolution to acquire territory in Spanish Flanders in 1667–1668, it seems clear that whoever originated the idea, the method was the King's own.

This idea was to make use of the rather complicated structure of territorial sovereignty which survived from the Middle Ages in the countries bordering upon France.

The Treaty of Westphalia had stated, for example, that the sovereignty of certain places in Alsace was to be given to the French Crown with the exception of those to which other lords had immediate rights or cities which could claim an historical independence. There could, however, be considerable argument over which districts might claim thus to be exempted from French sovereignty and about which places might be termed dependencies or appendages of other districts that had in fact been handed over to France. By asserting his right to take up claims which had hitherto remained dormant, Louis XIV hoped substantially to extend his sway over Flanders, Franche-Comté, and Alsace. The three bishops of Metz, Toul, and Verdun were all under French influence and were induced to petition the French King to set up tribunals to adjudicate upon "usurpations" from their territory. Tribunals, known as Chambers of Reunion, were therefore created, the first one being formed from a committee of the Parliament at Metz in December 1679. Other Chambers were established at Besançon to deal with Franche-Comté, at Breisach to deal with Alsace, and at Tournai to cover Flanders. Far-reaching decisions were made by these Chambers which, since they all represented Louis XIV's interests, were in fact plaintiffs and judges in the same case. Territories formerly coming under the sovereignty of such influential nobles as the Elector of Treves, the King of Sweden, and the Duke of Württemberg were assigned to French sovereignty. The French King had kept some 140,000 men under arms after the Peace of Nimweguen and they provided a compelling argument in support of the verdicts of the Chambers of Reunion.

Louis XIV took care to buttress this method of extending the national frontiers with appropriate diplomatic action. Curiously enough, the most supine and valuable instrument of his expansionist policy was the Elector of Brandenburg, the great-grandfather of the aggressive Frederick the Great of Prussia. The motives which induced Frederick William to bind himself to Louis XIV were mixed, and included resentment against the Dutch and, above all, the Emperor who had taken certain Silesian lands away from him. The Elector may have calculated that since the combined military power of Europe had failed to check the French King's territorial ambitions, it would be more profitable for him to stand behind the big battalions and act, as a French historian has nastily put it, as Louis XIV's "Chargé d'Affaires in Germany." A series of treaties was concluded between Brandenburg and France between January 1681 and January 1682. By one of these treaties the Elector secretly promised to support Louis XIV's candidature to the Imperial throne. Since the Swedish King was one of the most energetic opponents of the reunion policy, the Elector also hoped that by firmly planting his feet in the French camp he would be able to regain Western Pomerania, which Louis XIV had withheld from his grasp a year earlier, Louis XIV also managed to detach Charles II of England from the Dutch alliance and was able to profit from internal English political difficulties that found their expression in the Popish Plot agitation. It is true that a treaty was concluded between Sweden and the Dutch Republic to defend the Nimweguen settlement and that later both the Habsburg rulers joined this alliance, but broadly the French King made his dispositions too quickly for the slow-moving machinery of international diplomacy to creak into action against him. The German Diet might raise 40,000 troops; the French King had thrice that number.

As a result of the fulfilment of "acts of reunion" Strasbourg was in the summer of 1680 the only independent state left in Alsace. The history of this great city was peculiar. Owing largely to its geographical position on the left bank of the Rhine, since at least the thirteenth century it had been virtually autonomous and outside the reach of German overlordship. Gradually it attained a status of independence not dissimilar from that of the Swiss Cantons, with which it maintained the closest relations. At the Reformation Strasbourg had come under the influence of both Zwingli and Calvin; the latter is indeed said to have been the founder of French influence there. In the

Thirty Years War Strasbourg was allied with France and received the protection of Louis XIV. During the recent war Strasbourg had been a neutral, but the city had been occupied by Imperial forces which withdrew, however, upon French request in August 1679.

The methods by which Louis XIV proceeded to subject and overrun this small but strategically valuable independent Protestant republic can scarcely be defended by impartial historians of a liberal turn of mind, even if they are lovers of France. A French historian, M. Legrelle, has devoted a fat volume to this question in which he attempts to set out Frances historical claims to the city and justify the French ruler's actions as a counter-blow to the menaces of the German Emperor. Historians writing in the twentieth century cannot avoid the comparison that springs to his mind with the technique employed by Hitler to take Prague or Danzig. There is a legalistic argument, for what it is worth (which is little), that the courts at Breisach had ruled that Strasbourg was assigned to French sovereignty by the Treaty of Westphalia; and it can be contended that the acquisition of the free city of Bremen by Sweden in 1666 constituted a precedent and an example. But the fact remains that an independent republic, which "belonged" historically neither to France nor to Germany, was first isolated by French diplomacy and then compelled to succumb to force.

Once the Imperial troops had been withdrawn, French forces cut the town off from outside help by dominating Alsace. Louvois forbade the magistrates to rebuild or fortify the bridge across the Rhine, which formed their only link with the Empire. The City Fathers had a clear notion of the fate that was awaiting them and sent a deputation to Versailles to interview the French King; the members received gold chains but no concessions. They pleaded vainly for their neutrality. They were warned that continued work on the fortifications or the admission of a German garrison would be treated by the French as a declaration of war. It soon became obvious that the independence of their city would be settled not by their pleas (any more than was the fate of Czechoslovakia in 1938) but by the decisions of the Great Powers.

In September 1681 Louis XIV took the plunge. A rumour that another Imperial army was on its way to the Rhine furnished the excuse. Strasbourg was invested by a French army of 35,000 men against which was opposed a garrison of only a few hundred Swiss. The Protestant burghers would have resisted if they could, but the city cannon had been spiked by orders of the magistrates. On the 30th the town capitulated. On October 20 the Cardinal Archbishop Fürstenberg returned to the see from which he had been earlier expelled. Three days later the French King himself arrived and after being greeted by the firing of three hundred guns heard *Te Deum* in the cathedral. On the same date Casale, a strategically valuable town on the borders of France and Italy (hitherto under the sovereignty of the Duke of Mantua) was seized by another strong French force. A little earlier French troops had occupied the county of Chiny, which belonged to Spain and lay between the towns of Metz and Luxembourg; the Spanish possession of Luxembourg itself was besieged in November.

How was the French King able to carry out with impunity these widespread seizures of other States' territory? The answer is that Louis fortified these acts of aggression by a masterly display of diplomacy. At the time when Strasbourg capitulated a conference proposed by the Emperor to discuss the French claims was about to meet at Frankfort-on-Main, the Emperor having failed in his transparently ingenious attempt to hold the conference in Strasbourg itself. Louis held out tempting baits to his opponents by offering to restore Freiburg to the Austrian Habsburgs, while at an appropriate moment in 1682 he voluntarily raised the siege of Luxembourg. Moreover, by means of bribes and other inducements five out of the eight German Electors had by 1682 become French allies. The Emperor Leopold himself was paralysed by menaces from the east. In the summer of 1682 Count Emeric Tokolyi, the Hungarian rebel leader, after a brief period of conciliation with the Emperor, signed a treaty with the Turkish Pasha of Buda, overpowered the German garrisons in Upper Hungary, and raised the standard of revolt once more. The closeness of Tokolyi's relations with Louis XIV is proved by the fact that when he first became the recognized Hungarian leader he issued coins with his name on one side, and on the other in Latin: "Louis XIV, King of France, Protector of Hungary." A far more serious danger to the Habsburg Emperor was the Turks. Tokolyi concluded a full alliance with the Turks and in the spring of 1683 the Sultan Mohammad IV and his Vizir Kara Mustafa, with an army of between 250,000 and 300,000 men, began an eventful march on Vienna. French historians have emphasized that although the Turkish invasion was so extremely convenient to Louis XIV at this time, no treaty had been made by him with the Turks and that he told his representative in Transylvania that he had no intention of allying himself with the Sultan. All this is true. On the other hand, the French certainly had secret agents operating actively in the Near East; Louis was throughout the ally of the rebel Hungarians who were closely co-operating with the Turks; and the Most Christian King made no effort, in spite of the appeals of the Pope, to help stem this dangerous Mohammedan invasion of Christian Europe. In July the Turks were at the gates of Vienna and the Emperor had fled. The French Foreign Minister expressed the hope that the siege would last a long time and finally fail. According to one account, Louis would ultimately have come to the rescue; meanwhile he consolidated his gains in the west.

French help for Austria did not prove necessary, for John Sobieski, the King of Poland, overcoming the intrigues of the French envoy at Warsaw against him, determined to go to the assistance of the Emperor. In September the Turkish horde which had encamped before the Austrian capital silently vanished into the night. This was followed by a declaration of war on France by Spain, resentful of Louis XIV's attacks on her possessions, such as Luxembourg, but the Spanish army was too weak to cope unaided with the might of France. Spain's only possible allies were the Dutch, but the Dutch had lost nothing directly by the "acts of reunion," and the Dutch republican party refused to allow William of Orange to declare war. In the late autumn of 1683 French troops occupied Courtrai and Dixmude, ravaged the country around Bruges and Brussels, and bombarded Luxembourg. In 1684 Louis XIV contemplated an attack on Holland and Hanover, but eventually decided to confine his war effort to Spanish Flanders. On June 4, 1684, Luxembourg fell to Vauban.

French diplomatic action and the Emperor Leopold's preoccupations prevented the Spanish army from receiving outside assistance. On August 15 the Diet at Ratisbon (the Frankfort conference had broken up without any result after fifteen months) agreed to a twenty-years truce. Spain also reluctantly acceded to this truce and so did the Dutch. Thus France was left unchallenged possession of Strasbourg, Luxembourg, and Casale, a large part of Alsace and Lorraine, and a number of villages in Spanish Flanders. The French King appeared to have reached the height of his power in Europe. But it may be argued that his position was in fact far less secure in 1684 than it had been in 1678. For the Peace of Nimweguen had been an agreed peace in which all sides had made concessions. The Truce of Ratisbon, on the other hand, was an armistice extorted by Louis XIV from his enemies only because a number of fortuitous circumstances compelled them to yield. But his inability afterwards to convert this Truce into a permanent peace treaty proved that its conditions were not acceptable to Europe as a whole. The aggressive and unscrupulous conduct of the French Government had indeed raised powerful potential enemies against him who, once their own immediate problems had been resolved, would be certain to take the first favourable opportunity to reverse a settlement which none of them regarded as permanent.

Louis XIV's way of meeting these coming dangers was to try to terrorize Europe into submission to his will. He had recognized and accepted the resentment of the Protestant Powers over the revocation of the Edict of Nantes, but in a way it satisfied his pride to see that the magnitude and ruthlessness of his decision were generally understood. He later extended this policy beyond his own frontiers by compelling the Duke of Savoy to "clean up" the Vaudois Protestants who remained in his realm and on whose behalf another European statesman, Oliver Cromwell, had once exerted his influence. Other smaller Powers were also obliged to acknowledge the direction of the long and strong hand of France. The Republic of Genoa, which was accused of assisting Spain against France, was bombarded into abject submission in January 1685. In 1683 and 1685 the Berbers of Tripoli were also bombarded by the French fleet, and a squadron was sent to Cadiz in June 1686 to furnish a weighty argument in a bilateral trade dispute. Even the Elector of Brandenburg, who now began to tire of the French alliance, as he discovered it was gaining him no profits, was temporarily compelled by French diplomacy to reaffirm his previous commitments.

It might indeed have seemed from Louis XIV's conduct of foreign affairs at this time that he was determined upon a fresh war, greatly though this would have been against his best interests. For he did not confine his habit of picking quarrels only to small and weak Powers. We have already noticed his dispute with Pope Innocent XI over the right of asylum in the French ambassador's quarters in Rome, which culminated in the French seizing the papal territory of Avignon in 1688. At about the same time two further opportunities for the expansion of French political influence presented themselves. One was the death of the Elector Palatine. Louis at once put forward claims on behalf of his brother's wife, Elizabeth Charlotte, who was the sister of the dead Elector. More important still the approaching demise of the Elector Archbishop of Cologne in the winter of 1688 afforded an opportunity to the French King to introduce another of his own creatures into the control of this strategic city. Louis's chosen candidate for the succession was Cardinal Fürstenberg, the same ecclesiastic whom Louis had earlier forced as bishop upon the reluctant Protestant city of Strasbourg. Fürstenberg could not, however, be installed without papal dispensation, which Innocent XI rigorously withheld. In spite of this bar to his election and although after the death of the Elector in June 1688 he failed to receive the requisite number of votes in the cathedral chapter, Louis XIV determined to make Fürstenberg Elector even at the point of French bayonets.

All these grave provocations to the peace of Europe were in the nature of blackmail. It is clear that Louis did not really want war. He knew, however, that both England and Holland were divided by internal political difficulties and that the Emperor was still distracted by his wars against the Hungarians and the Turks, and he hoped by all these threats or displays of armed might to force the acceptance of the Truce of Ratisbon upon Europe as an enduring settlement which would leave France in possession of the left bank of the Upper Rhine. Inevitably the German States began to draw together in self-defense. By the Treaty of Augsburg (July 9, 1686) the Emperor and certain other members of the German Diet (including the King of Sweden in the interest of his German possessions) undertook to defend each other if breaches were made in the Treaties of Westphalia or Nimweguen or in the Truce of Ratisbon. But the significance of this treaty has sometimes been exaggerated. It was purely defensive and it was not comprehensive since not all the German Electors adhered to it. Its main importance is that it showed the growing concern in Germany over the aggressive conduct of Louis XIV.

In France there seems to have been a sober realization that another war was bound to come. The notion, so dear to aggressive Powers throughout the history of the world, that war can be averted by menaces may have been nourished by the King himself; but war was not averted—it was scarcely even postponed. The French Council of State, relates, Saint-Simon, spent these years less in fêtes and rejoicing over their diplomatic triumphs than in "devotion and constraint." "Here," he added, "ended the apogee of this reign and the height of Louis XIV's glory and prosperity. The great captains, the great ministers at home and abroad were no more; their places were taken only by pupils. We now enter the secondary age . . . very different from the first."

Chapter 8

France Against Europe

ON SEPTEMBER 24, 1688, Louis XIV declared war upon the Habsburg Emperor. The omens appeared favourable and Louis considered that if he did not act then, the opportunity might pass. He declared that "he could not doubt that he would be attacked as soon as the war with the Turks had been brought to an end." And that did not seem to be a distant prospect. For in August 1687 the Emperor had won a notable victory at Mohacs and that very month his forces had taken Belgrade. Holland and England were distracted by an approaching civil war in the British Isles. The Germans were still divided. In his proclamation the French King condemned the Emperor Leopold for refusing to convert the Truce of Ratisbon into a permanent treaty, for forming the League of Augsburg, and for opposing his wishes over the affairs of Cologne and the Palatinate. French forces seized Liége, attacked Philippsburg on the right bank of the Rhine, and occupied part of the territory of the Elector of Cologne. Philippsburg surrendered on October 29 and Mannheim capitulated on November 12. Louis XIV's progress along these smooth paths of aggression was at first interrupted by only one disturbing, if not unexpected, event. In the first week of November William of Orange, his most dangerous enemy, who had been invited by the English aristocracy to unseat his father-in-law, James II, from his throne, disembarked unopposed in Devonshire.

It is a subject of historical controversy why Louis XIV deliberately decided to send his troops into the Palatinate instead of using them to prevent the departure of William and to threaten Holland, thereby saving the crown of his ally, the Roman Catholic James II. The French King had, however, many seemingly adequate reasons for his decision. In the first place James himself, proud and bigoted, had spurned the proffered help of the French monarch. Secondly, the French ruler had expected that James would put up a prolonged fight with his own resources which would paralyse both of France's Protestant neighbours indefinitely. Thirdly, since the main objective of the French King's policy was to consolidate his gains on the left bank of the Rhine and profit from the distraction of the Emperor, he did not want unnecessarily to provoke the Dutch. The miscalculation proved serious. For William of Orange won a bloodless victory and England ceased to be an ally of France—or at worst a benevolent neutral—and entered the camp of her enemies. Indeed France was served less well by her diplomatic advisers than she was by her soldiers. During the next few years the successors of Turenne and Condé, men like Luxembourg and Vendôme, had to wage war in the adverse conditions created by indifferent diplomacy.

Thus the easy initial conquests of the French army in 1688 were soon offset by inconvenient happenings abroad. William of Orange rapidly established his position in London and was declared King of England by a grateful Parliament. In February 1689 the Queen of Spain, a French Princess who had sustained the cause of Louis XIV at Madrid, died, and King Charles II was induced to permit German troops to garrison the Belgian fortresses, the French King being compelled to retort with a declaration of war. In May the Emperor and the Dutch signed an offensive and defensive treaty, to which England, Spain, and the Duke of Savoy later acceded, thereby completing the First Grand Alliance against France. England declared war in the same month. Thus Louis XIV, who had tried to blackmail the Habsburg Emperor into conceding his demands with regard to the Rhine frontier by a threat of force, found himself committed to a war against half Europe.

Confronted by so extensive a coalition from the outset, the French King determined to fight this fresh war by keeping to the defensive, by converting France into one vast fortress. by not undertaking any large battles unless they became unavoidable, and by leaving the initiative to the enemies of France, challenging them, if they wished, to hurl themselves against the ring of fortresses which the great Vauban had constructed along the frontiers. The first step taken to fulfil this strategy was to shorten the line, and a drastic method was used. It was decided to evacuate the Palatinate and by carrying through what a later age called a scorched-earth policy to prevent the Germans from thrusting across the Rhine into the heart of France. It is one of the ironies of history and a reflection upon the outlook of the seventeenth century, which used individuals as pawns to enforce national territorial claims, that Charlotte Elizabeth, the princess on whose behalf Louis XIV had asserted his right to interfere in the Palatinate, was the person most bitterly upset by this devastation wrought upon her native land by orders of her brother-in-law. The whole country was ravaged, the beautiful city of Heidelberg set on fire, and its castle destroyed. In those more humane times than our own even the French general charged with the execution of the devastation questioned its wisdom: "I must represent to his Majesty," he told Louvois, "the bad effect which such a desolation may make upon the world in respect to his glory and reputation." The exasperated peasantry of the Palatinate were driven to guerrilla warfare against the French troops, and since the same country had previously been devastated by Turenne this fierce deed of war was remembered for generations. Several German princes who had formerly been allies of Louis XIV and were the natural admirers and imitators of the Great Monarch, were provoked into forming a coalition against him. The Elector of Bavaria broke with France, and at the Concert of Magdeburg the Electors of Brandenburg and Saxony and other small States planned to dispatch an army to the Rhine. In spite of the devastation of the Palatinate Bonn and Mainz were reoccupied by the German forces, and farther north the Allies crossed the French frontier into Belgium and ravaged the cantons of Tournai and Flanders. In face of every diversion, however, Louis XIV wisely refused to carry out an undue dispersal of his forces. In Flanders and Alsace the French armies rigidly kept to the defensive, while the Duke of Noailles invaded Catalonia with the intention of knocking Spain out of the war. At sea a powerful navy under Admiral de Tourville threatened the English and Dutch lines of communication and commanded the Channel, thus enabling King James II and his French advisers to effect a landing in Ireland. Other daring French sailors, akin to pirates, led by Forbin and Jean Bart, successfully preyed upon the commerce of the wealthy maritime nations now closely bound in enmity to France.

With considerable advantages, such as a highly experienced army under a united command and a vastly improved navy, the strategy of Louis XIV in this war showed a certain degree of feebleness and lack of direction which must in part be attributed to the death of Louvois, who was succeeded by his dissipated twenty-three-year-old son, and to the death of Seignelay, who had done much to rebuild the French navy and had been replaced by the unwilling Pontchartrain. Only the cumbrousness of the coalition which confronted the French forces and the indifferent quality of the Allied generals, who commanded by right of aristocratic rank rather than of experience, saved Louis XIV from a dangerous military reverse.

We are fortunate in possessing an impartial account of the strategic resources of France written at this date (1690) by a German diplomatist, Ezechiel Spanheim, who had been living at Versailles for ten years. He tells us how the French navy had been improved by the reconstruction of the ports on which Colbert had lavished so much care—Brest, Toulon, Marseilles, Dunkirk: how France had a fleet of a hundred first-class men-of-war (these included twelve with eighty to a hundred and twenty cannon and sixty-eight with fifty to seventy-six cannon); how some 25,000 seamen were available from

whom sailors could be enlisted even although many
Protestant sailors had deserted on account of the persecution. On land Spanheim estimated the size of the
French army (including garrison troops) at 300,000.
He explained how the nobility supplied good officers,
while poverty, product of the inequitable system of taxation, proved a good recruiting serjeant for the ranks.
A weakness at this period appears to have been the
cavalry, particularly since France did not raise a sufficient number of horses and their importation was difficult
in wartime. The discipline of the army, he said, was excellent and the real admirals and generals—as distinct
from the members of the royal family who were sometimes put over them—were men fully schooled in their
profession by first-rate instructors. Not a great deal was
expected of the Lord High Admiral, who at that date
was the ten-year-old son of the King by Mme de Montespan. The army, however, served under discouraging
conditions; for in 1690 the French commanders in the
field were ordered by the Minister of War that "as to
giving battle or seeking the enemy everywhere—that
you will understand is unsuitable in the present circumstances."

Nevertheless, the year 1690 did not go badly for
France. Three armies were put into the field: one under
Marshal de Lorge operated defensively in Alsace; Lieutenant-General Catinat commanded on the Italian frontier; and the Duke of Luxembourg directed the campaign
in Flanders. A small French force supported King James
II in Ireland. In 1689 William III had sent 8,000 men
to fight in Flanders under the command of John Churchill, Earl of Marlborough. In that year both William himself and Marlborough had to contend with the Jacobite
army in Ireland, and although the Allies collected a
considerable army in Flanders, Luxembourg was able
to inflict a severe defeat upon it at Fleurus (July 1). Ten
days later de Tourville won a naval victory over the
Anglo-Dutch fleet off Beachy Head. Later in the year
Catinat defeated the Duke of Savoy at Staffarda, south

of Pinerolo, while the Turks occupied the Emperor's attention fully by retaking Belgrade. The only setback for French arms during the year was the defeat of James II at the Battle of the Boyne in Ireland, which took place on the same date as the Battle of Beachy Head.

In the following year Louis XIV took personal command of the siege of Mons. A French diversion against the Duchy of Cleves, which belonged to the Elector of Brandenburg, distracted the Allies' attention towards the Lower Rhine, and King William arrived from Brussels too late to save Mons, which surrendered on April 8. In the same year Catinat occupied Nice and part of Piedmont, while Barcelona was bombarded by the French fleet. In Ireland the campaign came to an end and with it Louis XIV's hope of diverting the English from their operations on the European mainland. Tourville was still successful at sea and inflicted losses on Allied convoys. In the summer of the following year (1692) the period in which the French held temporary command of the sea was finished. Tourville, obeying unwise orders given by Louis XIV himself, was decisively defeated by the English and Dutch fleets at the battle of La Hogue (May 29). This defeat shattered the French King's plans to invade England with an expeditionary force of 30,000 men which had been gathered for the purpose. Henceforward the English navy commanded the Channel once more and the French, with their fleet crippled, were reduced to following the naval strategy invariably adopted by a weaker Power, that of commerce destroying. On land, however, the French successes continued. Louis carried out his annual feat of taking a town: this year it was Namur, which fell on June 5, and again his troops had to fight a bloody battle in which once again William III was defeated. At the battle of Steenkirk (August 3) the French and Swiss infantry distinguished themselves, the Dukes of Villeroi and Vendôme marching with their swords in their hands to retake the cannon which had been lost to the German infantry on the right wing. King William III in the centre attacked too late and withdrew through the defiles from which he had come out to the attack. William was so perturbed by this defeat that he talked to his confidential friends of the need to make peace.

The victories of Fleurus and Steenkirk and that of Neerwinden in July of the following year were due to the able command of the Duke of Luxembourg. Luxembourg, who had learned the art of war from Condé, was now in his late sixties. In his youth he had fought against the King and in 1679 he was imprisoned in the Bastille for allegedly being concerned in the great poisoning scandal. His character is well observed by the Duke of Saint-Simon, who served under him but had no reason to love him: "Nothing could be surer than the grasp of M. de Luxembourg, no one could be more brilliant, more resourceful, more clear-sighted in the presence of the enemy. On the battlefield he combined audacity with a coolness which enabled him to perceive and foresee everything under the hottest fire, and under the most imminent risk of failure; it was there that he was great. As for the rest, he was laziness personified. He never took exercise unless he was obliged to; his time was spent in play and in conversation with his intimate friends. Every evening there was a supper with a few guests, almost always the same; and if there was a town anywhere near, care was taken that agreeable women should be present." This remarkable old man, who was little liked either by the King or by Mme de Maintenon and who Saint-Simon felt did not quite come out of the top drawer, died in January 1695. His death was a grave loss to his country.

The year 1693 represented the peak of French military triumph. Louis XIV increased the size of his army, created a batch of new marshals, and instituted the Order of St. Louis as a reward for valour. The King himself set out for what was to be his last campaign. Accompanied by the ladies of his Court, he went to the front determined, as usual, to signify his presence by the capture of an important town before withdrawing to the comforts of Versailles. Against the advice of the Duke of

Luxembourg the royal choice fell on Liége. William III managed to reinforce the garrison and posted his forces strongly where they could protect the town so that it could not be taken without a battle. Louis XIV declined to fight this battle, and in June, to the consternation of his officers but to the delight of Mme de Maintenon, he left his army for ever. On July 29 Luxembourg decided to attack the enemy at Neerwinden. The Allies were in an excellent defensive position with their flanks well guarded, but their troops were too crowded to permit room for manœuvre. First the French infantry and then the cavalry attacked with gallantry and were repulsed with heavy losses. Luxembourg had the advantage of numbers, having between 70,000 and 80,000 men against 50,000. An assault with infantry protected by cavalry against the Allied right proved to be the turning point of the battle, and the Dutch and German troops were driven back into a river where pontoons had been laid to permit their withdrawal. The Allies lost about 12,000 men, the French between eight and ten thousand. Like Malplaquet later, it was "a very murdering battle," better suited, it was said, to be commemorated by a *De Profundis* than a *Te Deum*. Later, in October, Luxembourg took the fortress of Charleroi.

That same year the French again occupied Heidelberg and again sacked and burned it. In Italy Marshal Catinat marched on Turin and inflicted a fresh defeat on Victor Amadeus, Duke of Savoy. But perhaps the most notable military achievement of the year was that Tourville attacked and captured a large part of an Anglo-Dutch convoy returning from Smyrna, the prize being valued at 500,000 crowns.

Nevertheless, at the end of 1693 the French King had shot his bolt and he knew it. After five years, war weariness began to be felt, and this was intensified by bad harvests which brought famine and discontent with them. The Allies, for their part, had found time to marshal their resources and expand their armies. A British fleet was sent to the Mediterranean, where its presence compelled the French to retire from the siege of Barcelona. Neither in Flanders nor in Germany were there any eventful actions; the Duke of Saint-Simon, who, owing to a dispute with the Duke of Luxembourg over questions of ducal precedence, had left that general's command, found time lying so heavily on his hands during this year's campaign that he began to write his celebrated memoirs.

In these circumstances Louis XIV tried to make peace; he opened negotiations by an official as well as by a secret route. At first he made his terms high, offering only to surrender his conquests during the present war together with Freiburg and Philippsburg, in exchange for the right to retain Strasbourg and Luxembourg. William III demanded the surrender of some of the Flanders fortresses which had been ceded to France by previous treaties or their equivalents. The negotiations broke down over this question of "equivalents."

The war continued in a desultory fashion for three more years. In 1695 Luxembourg died, an event for which Louis XIV attempted to compensate by the creation of twelve fresh marshals. Nevertheless William III managed to retake Namur, his one outstanding military feat in sixteen campaigns. The French King was seriously disappointed, for one of his natural sons had been in nominal command of the forces covering the town. It was on this occasion that he expressed his anger by breaking his cane over the head of a lacquey who had pocketed a biscuit and then informed his confessor that he did not consider this was an offence in the eyes of God. The King was justifiably upset, for the loss of Namur was the first real setback to French arms since he had mounted the throne. The event was reflected in his offers to surrender Luxembourg and to restore a portion of its ancient liberties to the city of Strasbourg.

It was French diplomacy which won a victory opening the way to peace in 1696. Victor Amadeus of Savoy, a State the geographical position of which invited its rulers to be turncoats, had come to distrust the aims of his

German allies. Secret negotiations were therefore opened
with France, the Duke demanding the towns of Casale
and Pignerolo as the price of his friendship. Louis offered to meet his requests, while not relaxing his military
effort. Catinat, who had been given power to act on the
King's behalf, "crossed the mountains in good time, and,
while maintaining strict discipline, threatened to devas-
tate the country, and especially to cut down all the mul-
berry trees in the plains." On June 29 peace was concluded, and by the Treaty of Turin (August 29) Victor
Amadeus changed sides, making an offensive and defensive alliance with France. This Treaty was worth at
least thirty thousand men to Louis XIV, and the Emperor,
whose territory of the Milanese was now menaced, was
compelled to agree in October to the neutralization of
Italy, much to the indignation of William III, who was
nevertheless inclined towards peace. He suggested that
the latest French proposals should be discussed at a
congress to be held under the mediation of the neutral
Swedes.

The reasons why peace came were, first, that both
sides were exhausted; second, William was taken aback
by the pacification of Italy; but, above all, the negotiations were made easy because after waging war for seven
years Louis XIV showed himself willing to offer every
conceivable sort of concession, including the surrender
of Luxembourg and Strasbourg, if peace could be obtained on no other terms. When d'Harlay, one of the
chief French negotiators, appeared at Ryswick with "the
frame of a skeleton and the face of a spectre," the enemies of France regarded him as an example of the
straits to which the French King's subjects had been
reduced; but d'Harlay retorted cheerfully that they must
not judge the situation from his personal appearance, for
if he had found time to bring his wife they would have
been equally struck by her ample size and high colour.
Probably the compelling reason which induced Louis
to concede his enemies' demands was the approaching
death of the King of Spain—or what seemed to be his

approaching death, for he lived three years longer. Louis hoped to lay claim in the name of his son to a substantial part of the Spanish Habsburg inheritance and, if possible, to acquire it by peaceable agreement. Hence he was conscious of the need for a friendly Europe. The reasons why he had made war in 1688, to extend his territory by imposing a reign of fear in Europe, had now lost their validity; and his deepest desire was not to threaten but to conciliate.

The terms of the peace were settled by two series of direct negotiations between a Dutch and a French representative. The first took place during the winter of 1696, and the second during the summer of 1697 between William III's favourite, the Duke of Portland, and Marshal Boufflers, in a number of conversations in obscure Flemish villages. A series of French victories, culminating in the capture of Barcelona, enabled the French King to extract slightly better terms than he hoped for earlier. It was eventually agreed that he should keep Strasbourg, although he had to give up all his other conquests and acquisitions obtained through the "acts of reunion" since 1678 except the town of Landau. Lorraine, which had been occupied by French troops, was restored to its Duke; Louis abandoned his candidates to the Electorates of Cologne and to the Palatinate; he made considerable commercial concessions to the Dutch, and agreed to their garrisoning a group of fortresses in the Spanish Netherlands; and he finally recognized William III as King of England. The capture of Barcelona made the Spaniards amenable to peace. On September 21, 1698, the Treaty of Ryswick was signed by France, England, Holland, and Spain; the Emperor Leopold, reluctant to recognize the French possession of Strasbourg, did not sign until six weeks later.

Louis, as M. Legrelle pointed out in his study of the Treaty of Ryswick, had deliberately made no demands on Spain, weakened though she was, for why should he as heir presumptive (through his first wife) to the Spanish throne bother to alienate his own heritage? He was careful not to compromise his or his son's claims to inherit in any clause of the peace treaties. He had written to one of his diplomatic representatives as early as October 1696: "Avoid above everything else holding out any hope of my renouncing in my own name or in that of my son the right to the succession to Spain." This "right," and his hopes of profiting from it, was the Will o' the Wisp which he was to follow until the end of his reign.

Chapter 9

The Spanish Succession

THE LAST SEVENTEEN YEARS of Louis XIV's reign were to be dominated by the question of who should succeed to the Spanish throne—a question which one French historian has indeed called the pivot of the whole reign. The prizes were glittering. For the Spanish Empire then comprised not only Spain itself and more than half of Italy but modern Belgium, Mexico, and the whole of Central and South America, except Brazil, part of the West Indies, the Philippines, Morocco, and the Canary Islands—in all, a handsome portion of the inhabited globe.

For two generations, since English sailors had defeated the Armada, the ruling power at Madrid had become enfeebled and had dissipated the fortunes made available by the early adventurers. While Louis XIV was creating the glory of Versailles the life flame of the Spanish Habsburgs "burned feebly in its socket." King Charles II, who had inherited the Spanish crown as a child in 1665, possessed but one outstanding characteristic, that of appearing to be dying for over thirty years. Although he was twice married he had no heir. He was nicknamed the Sufferer and came to live a life of melancholy in the gloomy Escorial palace brooding on the conviction that he was possessed by a demon. A monk who was sent for to interrogate this demon said that the Spanish King had clearly been bewitched from the age of fourteen. And not even a solemn exorcism carried through by a German Capuchin could banish the terrors of this wretched ruler of half the world. Although a struggle took place in Madrid between parties contending for the soul and what passed for the wits of the Spanish monarch, it is not surprising that the fate of his kingdom was discussed and settled at other courts by more balanced and far-seeing statesmen.

The French King had a double claim to be interested in the Spanish succession. His mother was the eldest daughter of Philip III of Spain (the grandfather of Charles II), and his first wife was the eldest daughter of Philip IV of Spain (the father of Charles II). It is true that both his mother and his wife had made solemn renunciations of their claims, but, in the first place, it was doubtful whether, according to Spanish law, they had the right to renounce them, and, secondly, the French ministers argued that Maria Theresa's renunciation had been tied up with the payment of her dowry, which was in fact never paid. Among other claimants to the throne was the Emperor Leopold, for he also was a grandson of Philip III and had married as his first wife a daughter of Philip IV. A daughter by his last marriage was married to an Elector of Bavaria and had a son by him, Prince Joseph-Ferdinand. Although there were several other candidates, the son of Louis XIV, the Emperor Leopold I, and his grandson the Electoral Prince of Bavaria had therefore the best claims to the Spanish succession. It was obvious, however, that the peace of Europe would be ruptured if either a French Bourbon or a German Habsburg were to ascend the throne of Spain. A compromise was essential, and long before the last miserable Spanish Habsburg passed away, Louis XIV proposed to divide the Spanish Empire by agreement.

As early as January 1668 a treaty had been signed between Leopold and Louis whereby the French King was to acquire Belgium and Franche-Comté if Charles II should die childless. This treaty was soon outdated by events. Thirty years later, with Charles II still childless and his life at last plainly approaching its end, the idea of a partition of his territories was again taken up by Louis XIV. This time he made his approach to William of Orange, who as King of England and Stadtholder of the United Provinces was the most powerful ruler in

Europe after the French King himself, and the most vitally concerned in preserving the balance of power. French diplomacy was directed with consummate skill. Louis XIV's ministers were well aware that the Maritime Powers would never acquiesce in a French prince succeeding to the rule of the whole Spanish Empire, or would even allow French sovereignty in Belgium. On the other hand, these Powers had recently reduced the strength of their forces, while the French had a large and experienced army still ready to take the field after the Peace of Ryswick. Consequently it was likely that the Maritime Powers might be persuaded into consenting to a French Bourbon acquiring some part of the Spanish Empire if they were convinced that this would not menace the security of their frontiers, for neither of them wanted another war which might be long and would certainly be expensive. Louis therefore began, like a higgler in a bazaar, by demanding a high price for not exacting his full claims. Then he offered a series of concessions. First, he suggested that the heir should be one of his younger grandsons, not his son nor the grandson who was likely to inherit the French throne, and he proposed that Belgium should be detached from the rest of the Spanish Empire and go to the Bavarian prince. Next he reduced his demands further; then he threatened to break off negotiations. Finally, he limited himself to claims in Italy but on behalf of his son, not of his grandson, since this alternative seemed least likely to provoke the fears of the English and the Dutch. The negotiations lasted many months. Eventually, in October 1698, it was agreed that the Electoral Prince of Bavaria, the weakest candidate, should become the actual King of Spain but that the Dauphin should take Sicily and Sardinia, the Tuscan ports and certain other smaller territories including the Basque province of Guipuzcoa, whilst the second son of the Emperor Leopold should acquire the Duchy of Milan. This arrangement would have meant that Southern Italy would have become a direct part of the French

Empire, a magnificent and valuable acquisition. The treaty was not accepted by the Habsburgs—in fact it was kept secret from them. However, King Charles II got wind of it and riposted by writing a will in favour of the Electoral Prince of Bavaria, who would thus have obtained the whole of the Spanish Empire, if he had the bayonets to make good his rights.

Meanwhile, in view of the essential importance of the Court of Madrid in his foreign policy, Louis XIV carefully selected a new ambassador to go there, who was ordered to report upon the internal politics and intrigues at the Spanish Court. The chosen ambassador was the Marquis d'Harcourt, reputed to be descended from a Bishop of Bayeux who was the contemporary of William the Conqueror. Harcourt was an affable and charming man with considerable experience of both warfare and court intrigues, the only blemish on whose character was said to be greed. His cleverness and loyalty were beyond question. Harcourt's instructions when he went to Spain in February 1698 were simply to report on the outlook. He was warned that were he to support the Dauphin's claim to the Spanish throne, he would "certainly start another European war." It may therefore be said that at this date Louis was sincerely determined on the policy of partition and had no hope that his son would rule over the whole of France and Spain as well as their vast overseas possessions.

But while his King was coming to terms with William III, Harcourt had an unexpected success at Madrid. He completely outmanœuvered the Austrian ambassador, who was a man without tact or skill. Harcourt made himself generally liked, entertained lavishly, attended bull fights, and gradually and discreetly built up a pro-French party. He had many obstacles to overcome. France and Spain were old enemies. The second wife of King Charles II was a sister-in-law of the Emperor Leopold, and pushed Austrian claims to the succession as best she could. But Charles II feared his wife rather than respected her.

When he sought consolation for the woes of his sickly existence he clambered down into the vaults to open the tomb of his first queen, a French princess, and gazed at her mummified features. Harcourt neglected no device to overreach his opponents at the Court of Madrid. But the strongest argument he had was the very might of his country. The desire of the wisest counsellors of the Spanish King was to avoid the partition and rupture of Philip II's Empire. It seemed obvious to them that if a weak ruler were to succeed, a war with France would follow, but if a French prince were called to the throne, then they considered that it was likely that the splendour and greatness of Spain would be preserved inviolate.

At the end of 1698, however, a partition of the Spanish territories seemed a certainty, for, in spite of Charles II's will, the Elector of Bavaria had promised that when his son occupied the throne in Madrid, the conditions of the Partition Treaty should be carried out. So everybody was temporarily satisfied, if vaguely uneasy. In February 1699 an unforeseen event shook Europe. The eight-year-old boy, to whom so magnificent an inheritance had been promised, died suddenly. The patience of the French King's diplomacy is well exemplified by the fact that no sooner had he heard the news of this death than he ordered his ambassador in London, Count Tallard, to inform William III that he was ready to discuss a new treaty.

The death of the Electoral Prince somewhat surprisingly caused rejoicing in Madrid; the Spanish King was personally pleased—perhaps his confused mind grasped the fact that yet another of his would-be heirs had predeceased him. No such feelings were expressed elsewhere in Europe. For the dangers implicit in the failure of a well-intentioned effort to avoid a fresh European war were only too plainly recognized. And now the two main candidates for the succession had been brought face to face; moreover, since the Emperor Leopold had just been freed from his eastern embarrassments by victories over the Hungarians and the Turks (a treaty was signed with the Turks at Carlowitz near Belgrade in January 1699), another European war appeared inevitable unless a compromise could be reached.

Louis XIV's new proposals seemed modest and suited to the mood of the moment. He offered to let the second son of the Emperor by his second wife replace the Electoral Prince as King of Spain elect. In return for this concession he asked only that the Duchy of Milan should be added to the Dauphin's share of the Spanish dominions; he was also prepared to agree to any solution deemed appropriate by the Maritime Powers as to the future of the Spanish Netherlands (Belgium). After four months of negotiations the Second Partition Treaty was signed between Louis XIV and William III in June 1699. By its terms the Emperor's second son, Archduke Charles, was to obtain the Spanish Netherlands as well as Spain itself and its overseas possessions, while the Dauphin was to exchange Milan for Lorraine with its Duke as well as to obtain the throne of the two Sicilies. This Treaty was only provisional, because the signatories wanted to obtain the assent of the Emperor, a requirement of first-rate importance to all concerned, since otherwise the main object of the negotiations, which was to avert war, might be stultified. The position of England and Holland was a little awkward. For by the terms of the Grand Alliance, which had been concluded between them and the Emperor in 1689, they had promised to support his family's claim to the whole succession. However, Leopold was now told bluntly that the Maritime Powers could not hope to fulfil this Treaty in the teeth of French opposition, since France was heavily armed and an unwanted war would be unavoidable if they did. In spite of the cowardliness of his former allies, the Emperor would only contemplate a partition which would have conceded either Mexico or Peru to the Dauphin and nothing more; he would not hear of the heir to the French throne acquiring Lorraine or any part of Italy.

He announced: "my situation would really be too miserable if we were to give France what she asks; hers would be too powerful."

In spite of the Emperor's refusal to accede, the Second Partition Treaty was signed by France, England, and Holland in March 1700. Louis XIV had thus won a notable diplomatic triumph. For not only had he acquired for the French Crown the promise of a powerful increase in territory and wealth, but he had induced England and Holland to underwrite the Treaty; they were now morally bound to coerce the Emperor and the Spanish rulers into carrying out its terms as soon as Charles the Sufferer died. On the other side, although the Emperor's son was to become King of Spain it was clearly laid down in the Treaty that the territories thus acquired by him might never become part of the Habsburg Empire.

The man in Europe most disappointed by the signature of this statesmanlike treaty was the Marquis d'Harcourt. Had all his patient work in creating a strong pro-French party at the Court of Madrid been in vain? He delivered a dignified protest to his master and left Spain for France. And yet, ironically enough, it was the very signature of the Treaty which brought his work to its fruition. The first reaction to the Treaty in Spain was a wave of anger. What right had these foreign rulers to settle the future of Spain over the proud heads of the Spanish people? The King lost his temper and the Queen broke the furniture. But second thoughts were cooler. "The Spaniards," wrote the Marquis de Torcy, who had now become the French Foreign Minister, "were generally of the opinion that this second treaty was a device used by France to intimidate them and to make them envisage the division of the Spanish Empire as certain if the Archduke was called to the throne. It was then commonly said that the only means of preventing the break-up of the Empire was to place it in the hands of one of the princes of the royal house of France."

The majority of the Spanish Council of State, headed

by Cardinal Portocarrero, Archbishop of Toledo, pressed for this solution. According to one account, even the Queen of Spain, who had quarrelled with the Austrian ambassador, was tempted to take the side of France by a promise made to her that she should be married to the Dauphin instead of being locked up in a convent, in accordance with Spanish custom, after the death of her husband. King Charles II himself was pushed by the logic of events towards the conclusion that his successor would have to be a Frenchman. For, as Sir Winston Churchill has written, "Within that diseased frame, that clouded mind, that superstitious soul, trembling on the verge of eternity, there glowed one imperial thought—unity." He began to look at the things of this world, wrote Saint-Simon, "in the light of that terrible torch which lights the dying." He sought the advice of his bishops and theologians: they recognized the French rights to the succession to a man. Next he consulted the Pope, who, after referring the question of conscience to his most distinguished cardinals, answered politically that the King must follow the advice of his council, based on the principle that it was necessary to preserve the unity of the Spanish monarchy. Charles II hesitated a little longer even after receiving the Pope's message. For it was a desperate decision to take. While he was still undecided, he was struck down by a fresh epileptic fit and the contending parties struggled for mastery over the bed of the dying man. At length, as autumn and death approached, he announced his verdict and on October 2, 1700, signed a will making Prince Philip of Anjou, the second son of the Dauphin, his sole heir. Failing Philip of Anjou, the Dauphin's third son, the Duke of Berri, was nominated as successor. But if the French princes refused the heritage, it was to pass to the Archduke Charles, second son of the Emperor. On November 1 Charles the Sufferer expired.

The decision taken by the dying King of Spain to nominate the Duke of Anjou as his heir was not the immediate product of French influence. The French ambassador Harcourt was actually not in Madrid at the time. It is of course true that the decision was indirectly procured by French diplomacy, and the correspondence between Louis XIV and Harcourt makes plain that Louis hoped for this result. But the French King had neither counted on it nor expected it. The tradition of Franco-Spanish enmity was too deep and too recent for any substantial hopes to be nourished. Thus there is no reason for supposing, as some of Louis XIV's enemies said, that he was insincere in negotiating and signing the two Partition Treaties. What he now did was to repudiate the latest Treaty which he had signed. He was not the first and certainly not the last European ruler to break his word for reasons which seemed convincing, indeed compelling, at the time.

When the news of the Spanish testament reached Versailles the King was about to go hunting and his son was out chasing a wolf. At a preliminary meeting called to consider the situation it seems that Louis decided to abide by the Partition Treaty. However, on November 10 he summoned a select council in the rooms of Mme de Maintenon to examine the problem from every point of view. At this meeting there were present Torcy, the Foreign Minister, the Duke of Beauvillier, who was governor of the King's grandchildren, the Dauphin, the Chancellor, Pontchartrain, and Mme de Maintenon. According to Saint-Simon's account, Torcy and Beauvillier were for the Treaty, Pontchartrain and the Dauphin for the will. In favour of the Treaty it was said that the positive gains of Lorraine and Southern Italy and also Guipuzcoa, "the key to Spain," would outweigh the doubtful benefit of having a French prince on the Spanish throne. For if the Dauphin acquired these territories they would ultimately become an integral part of the French Empire; whereas Philip of Anjou, if he became King of Spain, would (according to the terms of the testament) have to renounce his right to the French throne and might even become—as adopted rulers are wont to do—more Spanish than the Spaniards. At the same time the breach of the royal word might mean a long and exhausting war against not only the Emperor but also probably the Spaniards and quite possibly England and Holland as well. This war, said Beauvillier, might be the ruin of France.

There were, however, many powerful arguments on the other side. If the Duke of Anjou or his younger brother did not accept their inheritance the Spanish envoy had been ordered to continue his journey to Vienna and invite the Archduke Charles to take the throne: he would not refuse, and the Emperor would support his son by force of arms. The enforcement of the clauses of the Partition Treaty would therefore in any case mean a war against the Habsburgs, while in spite of their signature of the Treaty it was highly unlikely that the Maritime Powers would wage war alongside the French. For after all had not William III devoted his entire life to resisting French aggrandizement? He was scarcely now going to fight to ensure it. Indeed, he had admitted that the primary object of the partition was to avert a European war. Once the war came his policy would be decided (so argued the French) not by his pledges but by his interests. Thus the upholding of the Treaty might well involve France in war on many fronts —in Spain, Italy, and in Germany—without the prospect of a single ally, a war which would aim at depriving Louis XIV's own grandson of his hereditary rights. The Dauphin spoke vehemently in support of his son's claim; this fat little prince, sunk in sloth and lethargy, announced that he would prefer to see his son seated on the Spanish throne than himself to become the sovereign of Naples and Sicily. The King is said to have asked Mme de Maintenon for her opinion and eventually extracted from her a few embarrassed words in favour of accepting the will. The King reserved his decision, but next morning announced his acceptance of the will.

On November 16 after his morning levée Louis XIV led his grandson, the Duke of Anjou (now seventeen years old), and Castel dos Rios, the Spanish ambassador, into his study and told the latter that he might salute his grandson the King of Spain. The ambassador fell on his knees and paid a long compliment in Spanish. The King told him that Philip could not yet understand the language and that he must answer for him, which he did in excellent Spanish. Then, opening the doors which led from his study into the Court, he said to the crowd there: "Gentlemen, here is the King of Spain. His birth called him to the throne, the late King confirmed him in his rights by his testament, the whole nation has asked for him and demanded my immediate approval: it is the command of Heaven; I have obeyed it with pleasure." Then turning to his grandson, he said: "Be a good Spaniard—that is your first duty; but remember that you were born a Frenchman and that it is your duty to cement the union between the two nations; that is the way to make them happy and to preserve the peace of Europe."

Torcy addressed a Note to the European Powers justifying the acceptance of the will. He pointed out that the Emperor had refused to accept the Partition Treaty and that the Spaniards were determined to maintain the unity of their empire. Consequently the French King's preference of the will to the Treaty would ensure world peace. At first indeed it seemed that this would be so. It is true that the Emperor immediately decided in favour of war, but he had first to find allies, for he was ill prepared to fight alone. The English and Dutch peoples were most disinclined to fight. Indeed, the House of Commons launched a violent attack upon the signatories of the Partition Treaty. William III, though indignant, recognized that he could only change the public temper gradually and the Governments of both these nations were obliged to recognize Philip of Anjou as King of Spain. So also did the Pope, the Duke of Savoy, the King of Portugal, and the Elector of Bavaria, who hastened to convey congratulations and assurances of goodwill to Louis XIV. No European observer could at that moment have believed that the French monarch had made a wrong decision. As Mme de Maintenon wrote in her private correspondence, many wise people were then convinced that there would be no war over the French acceptance of the will, whereas the enforcement of the Treaty would have meant "a long and ruinous war." And perhaps these judges would have proved right, had not the French King made a number of mistakes which once again helped to create a powerful coalition against him.

At the end of 1700, therefore, it appeared as if Louis XIV's foreign policy had reached the peak of its success. No one in Europe wanted another war, and the increasingly influential mercantile classes in Holland and England were thankful that Southern Italy and the Tuscan ports were not to become a possession of the French Crown (as the Partition Treaty would have permitted), for then the Mediterranean would have became a French lake with incalculable consequences for the merchants of the two Protestant nations. Even although Louis XIV's grandson was to become King of Spain, so the argument ran, the two Crowns were to be separated and might— who knew?—in the course of time have found that their interests were divergent. After all, the Spaniards had the reputation of being a proud people and might not take willingly to French tutelage. Now, then, was the time for French actions and behaviour to be careful not to give offence and for propaganda about Louis XIV's intentions to be most conciliatory. Instead of this the first step taken by Louis was to have letters patent registered with the Parliament of Paris in February 1701 preserving the rights of Philip of Anjou and his descendants to the succession of the Crown of France. Louis probably envisaged that if Anjou became direct heir, his younger brother, Berri, would take over the throne of Spain. This move was therefore excusable but provocative.

His next measure had far more serious consequences. At the time of the last war, in which Spain and Holland were allies, the Spaniards had permitted Dutch troops to garrison a line of fortresses in Belgium, including Namur, Mons, and Ostend, and the French had assented to this in the Treaty of Ryswick. Louis XIV now obtained permission from Spain to send French forces to occupy these fortress towns. The Dutch soldiers were surprised and interned. The Dutch public were furious and the Dutch Government affronted. However, they concealed their wrath, announced that they recognized Philip of Anjou, and demanded the release of the garrisons, to which Louis agreed. This episode provoked an almost equal degree of concern in England, since the main object of English foreign policy (as reflected, for example, in the Partition Treaties) was to prevent the French from obtaining Belgium and, if possible, to have such Channel ports as Ostend in the hands of a weak Power. A case could, of course, be made out for the French seizure of the fortresses. For if war was coming, it was far wiser to have them occupied by the French army, so that they could defend the land routes into Northern France, than by the Dutch or even the Spaniards. But the point is that war did not then seem inevitable and the risk of leaving the fortresses in Dutch hands might (as events proved) have been well worth taking. Yet it was a risk and the decision was admittedly a difficult one.

In the first week of December the adolescent King of Spain left France; he was accompanied as far as the frontier by his two brothers, whom he was never to see again. Harcourt, who had been made a duke in November 1700, returned with him, full of good resolutions to allow the Spaniards to govern themselves. But he soon found that these resolutions could not be fulfilled. For the leading Spaniards had virtually forgotten the art of government. Their methods were leisurely and their outlook superstitious. "In Spain," they said, "servants are not birds," and the new King was solemnly advised that he had best rely upon the two guardian angels with whom his high birth had naturally endowed him. Harcourt soon found himself the chief member of the Spanish Junta, while Louis XIV was invited and encouraged to take affairs into his hands. Henceforward the French King, now in his sixties, had not only to govern France and direct a world war, but also to rule Spain from Versailles. Orders were given that final decisions had to be approved by Louis XIV on all matters of Spanish high policy. His armies and fleets took up action stations to protect Spanish territory, and in some cases Spanish forces were generalled by Frenchmen. This conduct seemed natural and even inevitable, for in the interests of wartime efficiency surely an attempt had to be made to adapt the methods of French centralized administration to the needs of Spain? But this procedure confirmed the worst suspicions of the other European Powers, to whom it offered irrefutable evidence that Philip of Anjou's succession meant in fact, if not in theory, the subjection of Spain to France.

Louis XIV's final error of judgment was scarcely excusable. On September 16 James II of England died. By the Treaty of Ryswick Louis had recognized William III as King of England. Yet, whether for sentimental reasons or because he regarded the gesture as a pure formality, Louis proceeded now to recognize James II's eldest son, James Edward (known as the Old Pretender) as King of England. Though such an action was provocative in the extreme to the English people, it is fair to point out that by the time it was taken the English and Dutch had already signed (on September 7) a Grand Alliance with the Emperor Leopold which promised war if the three Powers were not satisfied within two months that the Crowns of France and Spain were to be kept separate and if the Emperor did not receive compensation.

As soon as the Emperor Leopold had learned of the proposed succession of a French Bourbon to the Spanish throne, he had sent an army into Italy under the command of his ablest general, Prince Eugene of Savoy, son of Louis XIV's former favourite, Olympe Mancini. Eugene had entered Italy by the Brenner Pass, crossed the neutral territory of Venice, and outmanœuvred the French army under Catinat, thereby threatening Milan. Catinat was recalled and replaced by the Duke of Villeroi, who was beaten at the battle of Chiari (September 1701) and compelled to withdraw towards the Po. Thus the Emperor's forces were already actively engaged against France when he signed the second Grand Alliance. The exact terms of the Treaty were:

(1) That there should be no union between the Crowns of France and Spain;

(2) That the Archduke Charles should be given the Spanish possessions in the Netherlands and Italy;

(3) That the Dutch should be permitted to occupy a number of fortresses in Belgium which they might garrison permanently to protect their country against French aggression;

(4) That the English and Dutch should keep any overseas territory seized by them.

This was in effect a new partition treaty to be enforced against France at the point of the sword. It is ironical that the Emperor, who had refused to sign either of the previous Partition Treaties with France—treaties which might have been put into effect without a European war —now committed himself to a war from which he was in the end to gain little more than he had originally been offered.

France was now therefore confronted with the prospect of a long and difficult war. Yet it is hard to act as a severe moral judge of Louis XIV's policy, as many English historians have tended to do. In every dilemma with which he was confronted there was a great deal to be said on both sides. Even his recognition of the Old Pretender, so irritating to English pride, took place after war had virtually begun. Nor was the object for which Louis contended an ignoble one. For too many years France and Spain had fought each other. The placing of a French prince on the Spanish throne promised peace and security. It is easy to be wise after the event. As Louis himself said, "whatever decision I take, people will blame me." In the long run—after over twelve years of war—Europe was compelled, even though France had been defeated, to recognize Philip V as King of Spain. The French people may have later blamed Louis, as he must have blamed himself, for the errors of judgment which he made on the eve of the War of the Spanish Succession. But by this date Louis had become a cautious and an experienced statesman. The aggressive tactics of his youth lay behind him. And the decisions which he took in 1700 and 1701 might easily have been taken by anyone in his situation.

Chapter 10

Disenchantment

LOUIS XIV in his sixties was still elegant, and upright as a young man. But his frequent expeditions on the hunting field and his daily walks could not check the consequences of a life of overeating; the signs of dyspepsia were to be seen in a flushed face. His mouth had long been toothless, his cheeks had receded. In his looks were soon to be detected the disappointments of the closing years of his reign.

It has sometimes been said that the French King had now to sustain an unduly weighty burden, but there is much exaggeration in this. It is true that Louis redoubled his labours as he accepted new responsibilities and that he tried to direct the new war as well as rule over both France and Spain. But his ministers and generals were far from being incompetents. He still commanded a magnificent diplomatic service and an experienced military machine. In the Marquis de Torcy, his Foreign Minister, he had a devoted and capable member of the Colbert dynasty. On the other hand, Barbésieux, the last representative of the Le Tellier dynasty, had died in 1701 and was replaced by the second-rate Chamillart as Minister of War and Controller-General of Finances. But yet, as in his youth, Louis felt confident that he alone was indispensable. He personally selected his generals, planned their campaigns, and corrected every important dispatch.

The strategy decided upon by the King was in the main defensive. When on May 15, 1702, England, Holland, and the Emperor made their official declaration of war, they and their subsidized allies, Prussia, Hanover, the Elector Palatine, Denmark, and other smaller States, had an army of about 250,000 men and two powerful navies at their disposal. Moreover, in John Churchill, Duke of

Marlborough, and Prince Eugene of Savoy-Carignan they had military leaders of outstanding quality. France had a smaller army and only five allies, Spain—more of a responsibility than an asset, Bavaria, Cologne, the Duchy of Savoy, and Portugal. By the end of the following year both the last two States had changed sides. The French ruler hoped that if he could impose delay upon the enemy coalition and prevent its armies from breaking through into any vital territory, the Powers leagued against him would in the end fall out among themselves and thus afford an opportunity for the French diplomatic service to conclude treaties which would at any rate leave the bulk of the Spanish Empire in Bourbon hands.

The lands which the French forces had to defend were extensive. Not only had the vulnerable French frontiers to be guarded but Spain itself was open to attack from the Maritime Powers, whose navies commanded the seas. The Spanish possessions in Italy were equally exposed, not merely to assault from the sea but to land attack from Austria—indeed, Eugene's troops soon came within reach of Milan. With such massive commitments there would clearly have been no real chance for the French armies to take the offensive. The best that they could expect was to impose checks upon the allied armies wherever a favourable opportunity presented itself. And in the first years of the war this often happened.

To Italy, where the threat seemed most imminent, Louis XIV dispatched his grandson, now King Philip V of Spain, to show himself to his Italian subjects; there he joined the competent but lazy Duke of Vendôme with some Spanish troops. Eugene, who had been besieging Mantua, was compelled to withdraw, and suffered a setback at the battle of Luzzara (August 15). While the new Spanish King was out of his country an Allied fleet was sent to attack Cadiz. Although this attempt failed, a Spanish treasure fleet was either seized or destroyed, together with its French escort, in Vigo Bay. This action was too close to Portugal to make the Portuguese King feel comfortable and was a principal factor in inducing him to abandon the French alliance. The chief French successes took place in Germany. The Elector of Bavaria, Max Emanuel, who considered that he had by hereditary right substantial claims to the Spanish monarchy, was never entirely trusted by the French. According to a French lieutenant-colonel, many of the officers in the Bavarian army "hated all our nation" and would have much preferred "to take up arms" against France, against which country they had served all their lives and thus contracted an irreconcilable hatred against her." However, the Elector proved a useful and faithful ally. By concealing his intention he had been able to seize the independent town of Ulm on the Danube. This threatened the communications of the Imperialist army which was besieging Landau as a preliminary to the invasion of Alsace, while a French army under Catinat had been looking on impotently. After Prince Louis of Baden, the Imperial commander, had taken Landau he was therefore compelled to recross the Rhine. But he was soon attacked by another French army under Lieutenant-General Louis-Hector de Villars. Villars was an able, daring, and confident soldier who, now aged fifty, had already had a successful and distinguished career in the French army, rising from being a brilliant cavalry officer to become a Marshal of France. He had also obtained valuable experience as a diplomatist, notably in Vienna, and felt that he had not yet received his deserts for his services to the French Crown. The memoirs of his life are boastful and inaccurate, but probably reflect the spirit of the man. He records how in 1704, when he was left without a command, he said to Villeroi, one of the French "generals by favour": "I do not know whether the King will leave me without a command. If that happens, I shall have enemies at Court who will rejoice. But the enemies of the King will rejoice even more." In 1702 he was given a detachment from Catinat's army with instructions to cross the Rhine and link up with the Elector of Bavaria. Leaving Strasbourg late in September, he forced the river by a bridge of boats under the cover of artillery fire and inflicted a check upon the superior army of Louis of Baden at Friedlingen (October 14)—a battle in which the Imperialist cavalry were defeated and the French infantry withdrew. It was said of this battle that "both sides claimed the victory because both were defeated." Villars was unable to join the Elector of Bavaria but was rewarded for his achievements with the command of the army of Germany which he took over from Catinat.

Thus the French had a fairly satisfactory campaigning season in 1702. The only failure was in Flanders, where a new comet had arisen in the person of Marlborough, who was confronted by the conscientious but aging Marshal de Boufflers. The French troops, which were not intended (as some English historians have said) to invade Holland but to act on the defensive, were compelled to withdraw from the line of the Meuse and the lower Rhine, but still maintained their fortress positions in Belgium.

Villars was not content to rest upon his laurels during the winter of 1702-3. In January he gathered his troops at Strasbourg, again crossed the Rhine and laid siege to the fortress of Kehl. Having thus cleared his path to Bavaria, he withdrew into winter quarters to emerge in the spring, when, after by-passing the fortified lines of Stolhofen, where Louis of Baden had hoped to bar his advance, he rapidly joined the Elector of Bavaria in Tuttlingen. Tallard, formerly the French ambassador in London, was left with a corps to watch Louis of Baden at Stolhofen. Thus three French armies stood upon Bavarian soil. Villars now put forward a daring project. He urged that the combined armies should advance along the Danube valley, where they would link up with Vendôme's army coming from Northern Italy through the Tyrol, and launch together a direct attack on Vienna.

Meanwhile, in Flanders, Villeroi (transferred from Italy) and Boufflers, the two French generals who had failed to distinguish themselves in the previous campaign, had been unable to prevent Marlborough from overrunning the Electorate of Cologne and taking Bonn. Marlborough, who may have had some inkling of Villars's grand design, had a grand design of his own by way of riposte. His plan was to hold Villeroi's main army immobile while an attack was made by Dutch generals on either Antwerp or Ostend. However, this complicated manœuvre went astray and a Dutch army was defeated at the battle of Eckeren (July 2).

Villars' plans also went wrong. The Elector of Bavaria obstinately insisted on first marching into the heart of the Tyrol instead of following the direct route to Vienna. He entered Innsbruck unopposed, but he had dangerously stretched his lines of communication through mountainous and hostile country, and Vendôme failed to reach the agreed rendezvous. Before Vendôme could arrive the Elector of Bavaria had been compelled to retire to his own country along a narrow and precipitous road, harassed by the Tyrolese mountaineers. Meanwhile the armies of the Empire had moved into Bavaria, and Louis of Baden, by occupying Augsburg, threatened to cut off the army of Villars from its base. As soon as the Elector returned, however, Villars turned the tables and inflicted a defeat on the German army, which had come out to reinforce Louis of Baden at the first battle of Höchstädt (September 20). This defeat obliged Louis of Baden to abandon the city of Augsburg and to retire into the Black Forest. Louis of Baden's withdrawal also enabled Tallard to retake Landau, the sole fruit of the Emperor's exertions in Western Germany.

While Villars and Tallard were winning these important successes, the main damage to the French cause in 1703 was done in the diplomatic field. Victor Amadeus of Savoy deserted his ally (to whom he was also connected by marriage) just as he had changed sides suddenly and secretly during the previous war. This event weakened the French position in Italy, and the Austrian army commanded by Starhemberg (who had replaced Eugene) was able to link up with the forces of Savoy. The King of Portugal likewise changed sides, a defection which injured the French plan for the defence of Spain, for it offered the Allies a base from which they could attack Castile.

The Archduke Charles, the Austrian claimant to the Spanish throne, was thus enabled to land near Lisbon in February 1704, supported by British and Dutch troops.

In spite of the potential dangers in Spain and Italy the outlook for the French King at the beginning of the year 1704 seemed bright. His defences on his north-east frontier, where his troops had been ordered to act defensively, were intact. On the Upper Rhine Tallard's army held Prince Louis of Baden in check. The Franco-Bavarian army on the Danube directly menaced the Imperial capital, while the Emperor's attention was distracted by the revived activities of the Hungarian rebels who were overrunning Silesia and Moravia. In Italy Vendôme's army outnumbered that of Starhemberg. Even in Spain Louis XIV was able to revive the drooping spirits of his grandson's subjects by sending the Duke of Berwick, that "great devil of an Englishman," who because he was the illegitimate son of James II served the French Crown with distinction, to lead an Army into Portugal. But this was one of the years in military history when individuals counted for more than resources; and Louis's enemies had the advantage in commanders. Marlborough, disgusted with the restrictions that had been imposed upon his strategy by his Dutch colleagues in Flanders, made up his mind that spring to go to the rescue of the Emperor. Prince Eugene, who had been kept in Vienna during 1703 as president of the Imperial Council of War, decided in this hour of peril to meet him. Together they would try to conquer Bavaria and destroy the French army on the Danube, which, with its immense line of communications and shortage of supplies and equipment, offered a tempting prey. France, on the other hand, was deprived of the services of her best general on this crucial front. During the closing months of the previous campaign the antagonism between Villars and the Elector of Bavaria, long latent, came to the surface. The Elector demanded and obtained Villars's recall and Villars, himself sick of the Elector's obstructions to his plans, was not sorry to go. Louis, instead of finding him another command at the

front, sent him to deal with the Huguenot peasants in the
Cevennes who, provoked by persecution, had broken into
rebellion in 1702.

Villars was replaced by Count Marsin, an efficient but
uninspired officer who was said to owe his position to the
"cabal of dévots" headed by Mme de Maintenon at Versailles. The Elector awaited the arrival of Marlborough
and his army in the neighbourhood of Augsburg. First, it
was hoped that Villeroi would be able to prevent the
English Duke from leaving Flanders. Then it was expected
that Tallard would be able to stop Louis of Baden from
joining Marlborough. Both these hopes were disappointed.
On July 1 the Anglo-German forces approached the
Danube at Donauwörth. The speed of their advance surprised the Bavarians and, instead of being confronted by
the whole strength of their enemies in the strongly fortified
position of the Schellenberg fortress which guarded the
Donauwörth crossing, the Duke of Marlborough and
Prince Louis of Baden had to deal only with a detachment. The losses on both sides in the battle which followed
were formidable. But the Elector of Bavaria had to
abandon the system of defending his country along the
north bank of the Danube. He retired to his secondary
position at Augsburg, where he was compelled helplessly
to watch the devastation of Bavaria—the firing of crops,
the destruction of villages, and the seizure of stocks by his
enemies.

Nevertheless, the Elector of Bavaria—now the unique
ally of France and Spain in the whole of the western world
—refused to abandon the French alliance. One reason for
his refusal to do so was that he knew Tallard was on his
way to reinforce him. Tallard joined him on August 7 and
on August 11 Prince Eugene joined Marlborough some
miles farther down the Danube. The united French and
Bavarian forces, which now numbered about 56,000 men,
did not expect to be attacked. They were entrenched on
the Blenheim plain in the same area where Villars had
won the battle of Höchstädt in the previous year. Tallard's
forces were posted to the right of the line (in the neigh-

bourhood of Blenheim village), the Elector and Marsin
had their troops posted on the left. The centre was thus
weakly held and inadequately controlled. It was covered
by a muddy stream which, it was believed, would be difficult to cross. Nevertheless by the use of fascines, pontoons, and planks the stream and surrounding marsh were
negotiated by the Allied forces. Marsin attacked on the
left, but fierce assaults by the Allies on the French wings
protected this daring and unusual penetration of the
centre. The Elector and Marsin withdrew fighting in
fairly good order, but Tallard's army on the right was virtually annihilated, twenty-seven battalions and twelve
squadrons, which had been crowded into Blenheim village, being taken prisoner almost to the man. The French
lost between 20,000 and 30,000 men, and Tallard himself
was taken prisoner.

This was the first serious defeat inflicted upon French
arms during the whole reign of Louis XIV. The news
reached France first in unofficial letters. No one dared tell
the King. At length Mme de Maintenon was deputed to
inform him that he was no longer invincible. The most
detailed account was brought in person by the Marquis of
Silly, a brigadier who was taken prisoner along with Tallard and had been released on parole by Marlborough.
The King saw him one day walking in the gardens of Versailles without his sword. "What are you doing without
your sword?" demanded Louis angrily. "Sire," came the
reply, "I am a prisoner." The French were not accustomed
to bad news and, as the reports of casualties accumulated,
public consternation was widespread. It happened that at
that date a great-grandson had been born to the King. And
it did not improve the public temper when it appeared
that none of the festivities and fireworks in celebration of
this event was cancelled.

The campaign in the west ended with the recapture of
Landau by Louis of Baden, who had been excluded by
his two colleagues from taking part in the battle of Blenheim. After retaking Ulm and covering the first stages of
the siege of Landau, Marlborough had returned to the

Moselle where he occupied the towns of Trier and Trar-
bach with a view to invading France during the next
campaigning season. The only bright spot on the French
horizon was the successful invasion of Portugal by Berwick; but he was forced to retire owing to the sufferings
of his troops from the heat and from shortage of supplies.
Nine days before the battle of Blenheim a British fleet
had captured the Rock of Gibraltar.

The disaster on the Danube had shaken the French
King, who made tremendous efforts to stage a recovery in
1705. Besides maintaining his armies in Italy and Spain,
he put three large armies into the field on the western
front. Villeroi (now joined by the dispossessed Elector of
Bavaria) continued to direct the campaign in Flanders,
and Marsin in Alsace; on the crucial Moselle front Louis
XIV righted his mistake of the previous year by placing
Villars in command. He sent for this able and sensitive
soldier and soothed him with affable words and the title
of duke. Villars remarked sourly upon the hypocritical
congratulations of the courtiers and then embarked upon
a personal reconnaissance of the front.

Louis intended that his armies should stay upon the
defensive. A large-scale Allied attack was expected either
in Flanders or on the Moselle, and the French armies were
ordered to reinforce each other as necessity required.
Villars was convinced from the elaborate supply arrangements at Trier and from the activity of barges on the
Rhine that the Duke of Marlborough was planning an
advance into Lorraine, which, if it were successful, would
outflank the line of French-held fortresses in Belgium. The
preliminaries to the fighting were instinct with old-world
courtesy. Early in June Marlborough sent a message to
Villars saying that he was marching at the head of an
army of 110,000 men and expected to see a good campaign; he also sent the French general a present of wine
and cider. Villars returned these compliments and ex-
changed presents, while entrenching himself in an excellent
position. He also took care to strip the surrounding country so as to prevent his opponents from living off the land.

Partly owing to administrative difficulties and partly to some exceptional weather and the failure of his colleague, Prince Louis of Baden, to arrive on time with reinforcements, Marlborough was finally compelled to withdraw. His absence from Flanders had given Villeroi the opportunity to besiege Liége. Marlborough returned to Flanders and raised the siege of Liége, but this enabled Villars to retake Trier. Villeroi was forced to uncover Louvain, after Marlborough had outflanked his prepared positions on the river Dyle (July 18), but the expected battle did not materialize. Louis XIV, while not blaming his general, hinted at the desirability of more offensive action:

> The disorder which had befallen you (he wrote) springs from the dispositions of your army, which are consequent upon the great stretch of country you have to guard. I blame you in no way for what has happened but, our affairs having definitely changed their character, we must forget a kind of warfare which is suited neither to the genius of the nation nor to the army you command—at least as numerous as that of the enemy.

Villars showed a great deal more aggressiveness on the Upper Rhine, although Louis of Baden momentarily threw off his habitual sluggishness and achieved a minor success. In Italy, after an indifferent beginning to the campaign, the Duke of Vendôme had stopped Prince Eugene's advance to succour the turncoat Victor Amadeus of Savoy at the battle of Cassano (August 16). After the Austrians had withdrawn into the Tyrol Vendôme was able to turn his full strength against Victor Amadeus, and at the end of the year French troops had occupied almost the whole of his country except his capital Turin. The only serious setback to the French cause in 1705 was the loss of Barcelona (October 9), where the Catalans had rallied to the cause of the Archduke Charles. A French officer felt able to write:

> The last campaign has been so favourable to France

that she became convinced the wheel of Fortune was turning in her favour.

But Louis was not unduly elated and made his first tentative peace proposals by approaching the Dutch with offers of commercial advantages and territorial compensation for the Archduke Charles; but he unwisely failed to tempt them with substantial concessions in the country most coveted by them, Belgium.

The year 1706 was one of almost unmitigated disaster for French arms. In Spain a French army under Tessé failed to retake Barcelona and was compelled to retreat into France. The whole of Catalonia and Valencia declared themselves in favour of the Austrian claimant. Three Allied armies were concentrated against Madrid. On June 25 a mixed Anglo-Portuguese force entered the Spanish capital, where the Archduke Charles was crowned. The Duke of Berwick was summoned urgently from France (whither he had been sent back at Philip V's request before the fall of Barcelona) and compelled the Allies to evacuate Madrid. In Italy Prince Eugene waged a victorious campaign. Marsin, who was sent to replace Vendôme as commander of the army covering the siege of Turin, took up his new post with the most gloomy forebodings, which were quickly realized. At the battle of Turin (August 28) Marsin was killed and subsequently the French evacuated the whole of the Milanese. But the most striking French defeats were in Flanders.

The French army in Flanders was still under the command of Villeroi, who, smarting under Louis XIV's criticisms of his previous defensive strategy, determined to meet his enemy in battle. In May he marched out from his positions covering Louvain and confronted Marlborough's army by the village of Ramillies. The French left was protected by streams and bogs, but remembering the British advance across the stream at the battle of Blenheim, Villeroi was sensitive about the possibility of a threat to this flank, and his fears seemed confirmed by an early assault from the Allied right. However, Marlborough later drew off some of his cavalry from his right and thrust it against the French right, concealing this movement by using the fold of a hill between the two lines. The reinforced English cavalry, having driven in the French right, wheeled and attacked the left. The French fled, losing five thousand men. "It was on May 23rd, the Day of Pentecost," wrote a French colonel who took part in the battle, "that this action took place, as fatal to France and Spain alike as was the Battle of Blenheim, and although the number who perished on the field was not excessive, the losses it brought in its train later on were almost as considerable." One by one the chief Belgian towns fell, almost without resistance. Brussels, Louvain, Malines, Antwerp, Bruges, and Oudenarde surrendered. In July Ostend was taken. By August the Allies had laid siege to Menin, a frontier fortress in France itself.

Louis XIV sent for Villeroi, but did not reproach him. "Monsieur le Marechal," he said to the sixty-year-old magnifico, "we are not lucky at our age." Nevertheless he ordered Marshal Vendôme to come from Italy to replace him. Vendôme, a descendant on the wrong side of the blanket of Henry of Navarre, and a Prince of proud manners and dirty habits, rallied his troops on a new line covering Lille and Armentières. But to stabilize this front Louis XIV had been obliged to strip all the others. In particular Villars, who had begun the campaign with a minor victory on the Upper Rhine, was reduced to inactivity.

The losses of Catalonia, Valencia, Turin, and the whole of Belgium in one year had put the French King in a desperate situation. In vain he again and more determinedly approached the Dutch with an offer of peace terms, recognizing for the first time that his grandson could not hope to hold both Spain and Italy and that the Dutch must be placated with a fortress barrier in Belgium. When his offers were rejected, he prepared to retrieve the military misfortunes of the previous year as best he could.

Louis XIV had a substantial advantage over his opponents in that he was the effective supreme commander of both French and Spanish armies, while the coalition's strategic plans were always the result of compromise between equal Allies who all had differing and antagonistic notions of how to obtain victory. One consequence of the Allied dissensions was that the Iberian peninsula was relatively neglected. The Dutch fought for their barrier, the English first and foremost for the security of the Channel ports, Victor Amadeus for the extension of his territories in Italy, and the Austrian Emperor for whatever he could acquire for his family without undue exertion. Out of the whole coalition only the Portuguese were primarily concerned over the conquest of Spain, but the presence of Portuguese troops in Madrid was scarcely calculated to reconcile the proud Spanish people to the rule of the Archduke Charles. On the other side, Louis XIV took deep and profitable thought over the government of Spain. Three years after his ambassador Harcourt had been obliged to retire through ill health in 1702, he had found an enlightened and selfless successor in Amelot, Marquis de Gournay, who instituted many important reforms and encouraged industry and the arts. A French princess, Mme des Ursins, a woman of outstanding personality who first acquired influence at the Court of Madrid through her friendship with Philip V's young queen, was also used to direct the Spanish government. Louis XIV aimed at reforming the Spanish administration by a process of centralization similar to that which prevailed in France and to eliminate the useless Spanish nobility from their powerful positions in the State.

On April 25, 1707, the Duke of Berwick, now restored to his command, won a decisive victory in Spain. The Allies had mistakenly divided their forces and the one-armed general Galway had, as Sir Winston Churchill wrote, "set forth, cruelly weakened in numbers but in considerable optimism," to take Madrid once more. He was met by Berwick, who had an army nearly twice as large as that of his opponent, on the plain of Almanza. Although the French suffered severe casualties in the battle that followed and Galway managed to withdraw about half of his army in good order from the field, this victory was of immense consequence. It disclosed the dangerous effects of Allied disunity in their war in the peninsula. It rallied the Spaniards once and for all to the cause of Philip V, and it secured the throne of Spain for the Bourbons. It also enabled the French reforms in the Spanish administration to be pursued. Afterwards Berwick was able to suppress most of the resistance movements in Aragon and Catalonia and to occupy the towns of Saragossa and Lerida.

A month later the Duke of Villars won another great French victory in Germany. He succeeded in piercing the elaborately prepared fixed defences on the east bank of the Rhine between Kehl and Philippsburg known as the Stolhofen Line. But lines are of no value unless they are defended, and the Marquis of Beyreuth, who had succeeded Louis of Baden in command of the Imperial forces, was incompetent. When Villars, after concealing his intention to attack by attending a ball at Strasbourg, sent his troops to assault the fortifications, they were easily overrun. Afterwards Villars entered Würtemberg and lived profitably off the country.

As a logical consequence of concentrating his main efforts upon the defence of Spain, Louis XIV had now resigned himself to the loss of Italy. He concluded a treaty with the Emperor in March at Milan, whereby he was allowed to withdraw all his forces—including all prisoners who had been lost—in return for the neutralization of that country. Some of the troops thus saved were sent to reinforce Berwick's army in Spain. Milan and Naples were thus lost to the Spanish Crown.

The Allied energies during this year were devoted to an attempt to take Toulon, and Marlborough hoped that this threat would compel the French to weaken their forces in Flanders and thus procure a double invasion of France from both north and south. Orders had indeed to be given to scuttle the Toulon fleet and Villars was forced to retire across the Rhine, but the Count of Tessé, who was in command of the defence of the naval base, carried out his duties skilfully, reporting his successes in burlesque dispatches written after the manner of Sancho Panza. Prince Eugene, who conducted the siege in a somewhat dispirited manner, lost 10,000 men before he withdrew. In the north Vendôme defended his positions with equal skill beneath the guns of Lille. This campaign therefore represented a real triumph both for the French generals and for Louis's over-all strategy. The disasters of 1706 had been in a large measure repaired, but in 1708 disaster was to return.

On the whole, the French plans in 1708 were still defensive. An expedition against Scotland, aimed at starting a Jacobite rising, was defeated largely by the elements. In Spain some progress was made, but the Allies still held Barcelona. In Flanders Vendôme—now, as the custom was, nominally under the command of a French royal prince, this time the youthful Duke of Burgundy, Louis XIV's eldest grandson—seized the initiative with a bold flank march to retake Bruges and Ghent and imperil Marlborough's communications with Ostend. The two armies came into collision at Oudenarde on July 11. Vendôme attacked on his right, but, owing to a misunderstanding, his left failed to support him—indeed it took comparatively little part in the battle but "looked on as if from boxes at the opera." Marlborough pressed his advantage with consummate art and the French army was saved from destruction only by the coming of night. Five thousand men were lost and Vendôme and Burgundy wrote to Versailles blaming each other for the defeat. After vainly trying to force Vendôme out of Ghent by ravaging the provinces of Artois and Picardy Marlborough laid siege to Lille, which was gallantly defended until October 22 by old Marshal Boufflers with a garrison of raw recruits and stragglers from Oudenarde; the citadel did not fall until December 9, when Boufflers was allowed to capitulate with all the honours of war and return to receive the unstinted gratitude of his sovereign. Ghent surrendered at the end of the same month.

The military defeats of 1708 were accentuated by a terrible winter. The cold was said to be "as intense in France as in the regions beyond Sweden." The rivers froze, the crops were ruined, the fruit trees and vines were killed. France itself was exhausted and stood on the edge of bankruptcy. The prodigious exertions made to fill the armies that fought in every quarter of western Europe and to sustain weak allies on so many fronts could never be repeated on the same grand scale. Casualties not merely in battle but from a dozen sources of wastage had undermined the French armies. The grandees at Court quarrelled and the generals blamed each other both in private and in public. In a bitter paragraph Saint-Simon placed the blame for the state of affairs squarely upon the King himself, castigating

> his blindness, his pride in doing everything himself, his jealousy of experienced ministers and generals, his vanity in choosing only such leaders as could not be expected to earn credit for successes.

France was indeed threatened with famine and many peasants actually died of starvation. For the first time in Louis XIV's long reign, since the crowds had burst into his bedroom at Paris when he was a boy, the rumblings of revolution were heard. It seemed in fact as if now he had reached the age of seventy his luck had turned and the sun that had shone so freely upon the French monarchy was waning. There was no alternative for him but to seek peace and save what could be saved from the wreck.

Chapter 11

Sunset

MANY INFORMAL CONTACTS had been kept by devious means for some months between France, on the one hand, and the Duke of Marlborough and Heinsius, the leading Dutch statesman, on the other, with a view to discussing peace terms when the time seemed ripe. Bribes had been offered to Marlborough and a secret correspondence had been maintained between him and his nephew, the Duke of Berwick, the English-born general in the French service. A busy-body of a neutral diplomatist had employed himself as an unofficial mediator between the Dutch and the French. It was thus easy for Louis to open negotiations.

As the spring of 1709 drew near the reasons for seeking peace became all the more compelling. The situation as seen at the French Court through the eyes of Mme de Maintenon was dismal in the extreme. Bread and money were the public needs: "misery will soon overwhelm us," she wrote; "you would be deeply moved by the sadness of the King and his entourage." Though Court balls were still held after Oudenarde "more out of policy than for pleasure," these proved vicious propaganda for the home front. The people began openly to complain: "They say it is for the King to begin to economize. All his expenditure is criticized: the trips to Marly, it is said, are the ruin of the State: they say he should give up his horses, his dogs, and his valets; they complain about his fine furnishings; in a word, they say that he should make the first sacrifices."

The sacrifices made by the King were those which cut him most deeply. The first representative whom he sent to Holland, Rouillé, President of the Parliament of Paris, had instructions to be ready to surrender the whole of the Spanish Empire to the Austrian claimant, provided that Philip of Anjou were compensated with Naples and Sicily; to concede to the Dutch a handsome barrier of fortresses in Flanders; and to make commercial concessions to both the Maritime Powers. The Dutch, however, acted only as the spokesmen of the coalition, which still held firmly together. They tabled sweeping demands. The victorious Allies took the line that no portion of the Spanish Empire could go to the French Bourbon claimant, and that France itself must be reduced to the territorial position which it had held at the time of the Peace of the Pyrenees (1659). The famines in many parts of France, accompanied by disease and by riots and even by demonstrations at Versailles, forced the royal Council to study these harsh terms seriously. At a crucial meeting at the end of April it was decided that every diplomatic surrender would have to be made to obtain peace. The French Foreign Minister, Torcy, himself offered to go to Holland to carry on the negotiations.

It is possible that the very sight of the Minister of the Great King arriving in Holland cap in hand caused the Allies to frame even more stringent proposals. For not only were the French asked to give up all the claims made on behalf of Philip of Anjou, to forfeit all their conquests in Germany during the past fifty years, and to include several French towns in the Dutch barrier, but the French King was expected himself to enforce the expulsion of his grandson from Spain, while if Philip refused to leave Spain within two months the armistice was to expire.

Torcy advised his master to reject this harsh ultimatum if "the state of your affairs will permit." The council which considered Torcy's report in June had little doubt about the answer that should be given. The King's only son and the King's grandson, the Duke of Burgundy—next heir to the French throne—were strongly against acceptance. It was then suggested that the French monarch should appeal directly to the patriotism of the

French people by summoning the States-General, a representative assembly of nobles, clergy, and middle classes which had not met for nearly a hundred years. Louis felt unable to break with the autocratic principles of a lifetime, but he wrote a letter to his archbishops, governors and intendants explaining the trend of the recent negotiations and appealing for the sympathy and support of the French people. The indignation of the French public at the humiliating terms demanded by the Allies was general. Thus the rejection of the Allies' ultimatum was a national act. The King's dilemma was widely appreciated and sympathized with. Even the Duke of Marlborough confessed privately that had he been the French King he would have refused the demand to fight his own grandson.

At this moment of peril, with the enemy deployed upon the frontier, unsurpassed efforts were made by all French classes, rich and poor alike. Villars, the only French general who had not been beaten during the present war, was put in command of an army in the northeast in replacement of Vendôme and went forward into battle full of courage, although impressed by the extent of his responsibilities. The veteran Marshal Boufflers, the hero of the defence of Lille, offered to serve as a volunteer under Villars, an offer which was gladly accepted. Men flocked to join the colours. Such soldiers as were left from the previous campaign were for the most part without clothes, food, or even weapons. Bread was made for the forces out of rye and oats. Corn was bought from abroad and extraordinary exertions were undertaken to manufacture munitions. The rich were asked to sell their gold and silver plate. "When I saw that I was almost the only man of my rank still dining off silver," wrote the Duke de Saint-Simon, bringing up the rear, "I sent plate to the value of about 1,000 pistoles to the Mint, and locked up the rest." The ineffective and uninspired Minister of War, Chamillart, was at last replaced by Voysin, who (said Saint-Simon) "had the one essential qualification without which no man was ever admitted into the Council during the whole reign of Louis XIV . . . a complete absence of any claim to good birth." Birth, however, had ceased for the moment to count. The French people were united behind their King, who was at his best in this hour of national misfortune, and were determined to stave off both defeat and humiliation. Ambitions had grown modest. "If we can get through this campaign with nothing worse than the loss of Tournai," wrote Mme de Maintenon, no doubt speaking the thoughts of the King, "we shall have done well."

The campaign of 1709 did not open until June. This was partly because the bitter winter had been followed by a cold spring which destroyed the crops and meant that the cornfields had to be resown. Moreover, the previous campaigning season had ended late and the abortive peace negotiations had delayed the redeployment of the armies. The forces of both sides were held up by lack of supplies. Louis XIV concentrated all his available troops under Villars so as to defend France against invasion. Villars took up positions covering a line of fortresses which still afforded protection to the north-east frontier. On his left were Dunkirk and Ypres, on his right Tournai and Mons. South-west of Lille, between the minor fortress of St. Venant and Douai, Villars stationed his army and built entrenchments, known as the Lines of La Bassée. The Allied generals recoiled before the idea of attacking the gaunt and desperate French army in its fortified positions and instead decided to clear the flank by besieging Tournai. The town held out until July 30, while the citadel did not surrender until September 2. After this the Allies turned to assault Mons.

Villars was by nature an offensive-minded general and he sought and secured permission from the King to try to interfere with the siege of Mons even at the risk of a battle. The risk was grave, for this was the last great army of France. Villars was able to maintain it in the field only by giving much-reduced rations to the men who were out of the line. On September 7 he broke up his camp and moved into a screen of forest which lay between the

two armies west and south-west of Mons. Villars occupied both the two gaps in the forest and put infantry
into the surrounding woods. Then he drew up his forces
in a concave pattern so that if his enemies tried to assault
his centre they would be overwhelmed by fire from his
wings. Marlborough and Eugene, however, attacked the
wings near Malplaquet on September 11. Villars had no
choice but to await the assault, keeping his cavalry in
reserve in the hope of being able to launch an effective
counter-attack once the enemy had overcome the entrenchments. This was a battle in which artillery played
a considerable part. Villars had eighty guns, his opponents a hundred, with which they contrived something of
a barrage before sending their infantry into the attack.
Boufflers commanded the French right, while Villars
directed the left. The Allied attack on the left was so
fierce that Villars had to move troops from his centre
as a reinforcement. On the right Boufflers inflicted a
real but not decisive check on the Dutch Guards. But the
battle was decided on the left where twenty battalions
under a British general carried out a wide outflanking
movement through the woods. Villars had to denude his
centre still further and the Allies were at last able to
split the French line in two. In trying to counter the
unexpected, dangerous, outflanking attack, Villars was
wounded. Boufflers, who took over the command, was
compelled to withdraw from the battlefield under cover
of a series of counter-attacks.

It was afterwards stated at the French Court that had
Villars not been wounded, the battle would have been
won. There seems little substance in this. Boufflers rightly
described the action as "unhappy but glorious." Heavy
casualties were suffered on both sides, but the Allies lost
a higher proportion of their army than did the French.
Villars had restored the honour of the French army,
raised the morale of his men, and prevented the invasion
of France. The Allies turned aside to complete the siege
of Mons, which fell on October 23. Both armies, completely exhausted, then retired into winter quarters.

Louis XIV had been able to concentrate his main resources upon fighting the war in Flanders because he had not only concluded an armistice in Italy but had left the defence of the Iberian Peninsula primarily to the Spaniards themselves with French advisers. The Allies had at the same time insisted that the Austrian claimant to the French throne should supply the bulk of the forces in this theatre. The King's nephew, Philip, Duke of Orleans (the future Regent of France) had distinguished himself in 1708 by capturing the town of Tortosa, which the Austrians failed to retake. In the same year Minorca had been lost to the Spanish Crown. Little happened in 1709 except for the capture of Alicante, a strategic town in Valencia, by the Allies. In 1710, however, the Spanish forces were twice defeated in Aragon (notably at the battle of Saragossa on August 28, 1710) and the Archduke Charles entered Madrid for the second time at the end of September. But his troops and advisers were confronted by assassinations, guerrilla warfare, and passive resistance. In Spain, as in France, the coalition found itself faced by a national patriotic movement.

Louis XIV had not been especially cheered by the battle of Malplaquet and had reopened negotiations with the Allies. The Dutch, who were now anxious for peace, had, however, been more closely bound to England by the Barrier Treaty of October 1709, which promised them virtually the whole of Belgium as a permanent defence against French aggression. Although the Dutch interviewed Louis XIV's representatives, they were the cat's-paws of the English Whig Party, which stood by the letter and spirit of the ultimatum of May 1709. At these negotiations, which took place at the small town of Gertruydenberg, the French King offered to hand over to the Allied armies four French towns as a pledge that he would in no way assist his grandson to retain the throne of Spain. Moreover, he stressed the fact that all French forces had already been withdrawn from Spain. He also offered a subsidy to the Allies to meet the expense of dethroning his grandson and he agreed to give up Alsace to the Emperor. Villars himself had urged the King to offer every possible concession. But Louis XIV again refused to levy war on his grandson in return for the mere concession of a two-month armistice. So the war had to go on. Villars, recovered from his wound, carried out a successful defensive campaign. For the Allied generals the shadow of the murderous battle of Malplaquet overhung all their actions in northeast France, for although Marlborough and Eugene had some 120,000 men at their disposal they were afraid to risk another battle. The only serious French loss in 1710 was the town of Douai, which fell at the end of June.

Allied diplomatic intractability and lack of military success in 1710 decided Louis XIV once more to send forces into Spain. The Duke of Vendôme was restored to favour and given an army raised largely from the garrison of Navarre with which to assist Philip of Anjou in his hour of need. Vendôme concentrated his forces by the river Douro and the Archduke Charles was again obliged to abandon Madrid. With an army of some 25,000 men Vendôme entered Madrid, and learning that part of the Allied army under the English general Stanhope had become detached from the rest, attacked it at Brihuega, making Stanhope himself a prisoner. Two days later (on December 10) a mixed French and Spanish army encountered the army under the Austrian Starhemberg at Villa Viciosa. On the first day of this battle the French right was victorious but the left was beaten; on the next day Vendôme returned with the horse of his left wing and set out in pursuit of Starhemberg, who had also withdrawn from the battlefield. At the battles of Brihuega and Villa Viciosa the Austrians lost 7,500 men and the cause of King Philip was finally restored.

By 1711 the whole world had grown weary of war. In England Queen Anne had tired of the incessant slaughter, and in a general election the Tory party won an overwhelming victory over the Whigs, who were deemed to be the war party. In April 1711 the Emperor Joseph (who had succeeded his father the Emperor Leopold in 1705) had died of smallpox, and his death cast doubt on the whole meaning and purpose of the war for the Allies; for his brother, the Archduke Charles, now was heir to the vast Habsburg dominions in Central Europe, and it became obvious that if he were to succeed to both the Spanish and the Austrian Empires this would destroy the balance of power in Europe. That was the outstanding political consideration; but the Emperor's death also had an important military effect. Prince Eugene and the Imperial army had to be withdrawn from France in order to ensure the Archduke's election as Emperor in Germany. This left Marlborough's forces inferior to those of the French and thus, although at the end of the previous campaign he had broken into the last line of the French fortresses and he now took the valuable town of Bouchain (September 1711), his wonderful military career terminated on a minor key. At the same time, when Archduke Charles left Spain to be crowned Emperor, the territory left under his control had been reduced to Catalonia, the "Ireland" of Spain. These events and the victories of Vendôme in Spain encouraged Louis XIV to hope to exact better peace terms than he could conceivably have obtained in 1709 and 1710.

In the same month that the Emperor died, the death of Louis XIV's only son also took place. The Dauphin was no credit to his father; he had been idle and inarticulate and was devoted only to eating, sleeping, hunting, and an ugly mistress. He prided himself on being the son of a King and the father of a King; he had little ambition for himself but much for his children. He had played his role in history by producing three sons of vastly different characters—the Duke of Burgundy, Philip of Anjou, and the Duke of Berri. The French King was delighted with these progeny, who promised an adequate and even distinguished posterity. Anjou, although unduly submissive to his womenfolk and said always to have his mouth open, had proved himself capable of both courage and loyalty. He was deliberately to renounce his claim to the French throne to keep his troth with his adopted subjects of Spain.

Louis's eldest grandson, the Duke of Burgundy, held out promise indeed. He had received an excellent education at the hands of the liberal-minded Archbishop Fénelon and the Duke of Beauvillier. Shy and diffident as a youth, Burgundy's interests were wide and his social conscience keen. His austere outlook did not commend him to his father, and he suffered some ill-deserved unpopularity for the part he had played in the Oudenarde campaign. His main interests were morals and metaphysics, but he also dabbled in the physical sciences. He contemplated many improvements and reforms when he became King. It was perhaps a misfortune for France that he did not live to inherit the throne. Burgundy's wife, Marie Adelaide, was as gay as her husband was grave; she was a princess "who animated everything and charmed everyone." Acknowledged leader of Court Society, she was up all night and every night. She was the King's spoilt child and few who knew her did not love her —her husband the most passionately of all. She bore him three sons.

The Duke of Berri was very different from his elder brother and took after his father in his absorption in sport and the more obvious pleasures of life. He was married to a granddaughter of Louis XIV's brother Orleans, who had died in 1701. Her father, Philip of Orleans, was a remarkable man. For although he had a rather unsavoury reputation in private life, he was a soldier of distinction and a genuine patron of the arts. His daughter imitated only her father's less admirable characteristics.

Louis XIV in his treatment of his family was a curious mixture of cold and heat. He showed himself totally indifferent to the deaths of his only brother and only son, just as he had been unmoved by the deaths of his most loyal and devoted servants. He forbade all elaborate mourning, and the gambling, comedies, masked balls, and hunts which were the staple of Court life continued throughout the tragic closing years of his last war. On the other hand, he rejoiced in the births of his grandsons and great-grandsons, and although he expressed no emotion over the deaths of his former mistresses, he lavishly spoiled his two bastard sons, the worthless Dukes of Maine (by La Vallière) and Toulouse (by Montespan).

In 1712 the King's indifference to mortality was roughly shaken by the deaths in rapid succession of the Duke of Burgundy, his heir, the Duchess of Burgundy, his favourite, and their eldest son, who was next in the line of succession. These deaths took place within three weeks of each other in February and March. They were followed two years later by the death of the Duke of Berri. Since Philip of Anjou had renounced the throne, a two-year-old child (the future Louis XV) was left as the sole direct male heir to the French monarchy. "The King," wrote Mme de Maintenon, "does everything he can to console himself, but always falls into the same state of sadness . . . Everything is lacking, appears empty; there is no more joy, no more activity." What a contrast for a Court where normally silence was never the rule except at mealtimes.

Nevertheless, the King bore these hard blows of fate with dignity. Even the Duke of Saint-Simon, who in the volume of his *Memoirs* in which he epitomizes this reign has little good to say of the King, cannot forbear a word of praise for the way in which the King confronted his public and private misfortunes. Louis had few old friends on whom he could rely—Mme de Maintenon and the Marquis of Villeroi, now restored to favour, were almost his only cronies. He thrust himself again into the work of ruling to save what he could from the chaos into which the war of the Spanish Succession had plunged his kingdom.

The death of the Emperor Joseph, with its repercussions on the European balance of power, had persuaded some of France's enemies to contemplate less onerous peace terms. After securing a contact through a French abbé, who had been chaplain to Marshal Tallard when he was ambassador to England, the French King offered proposals which were particularly beneficial to English commerce. These proposals were communicated in general terms to the Dutch, who expressed themselves as being in favour of peace. Louis then wisely concentrated on detaching England from the Grand Alliance. In the summer of 1711 the poet Matthew Prior went to Versailles as representative of the new Tory Government, and in October three provisional agreements were signed in London. One of them was kept secret. This provided for large concessions to England, including special tariff privileges for British industry, the transfer of Gibraltar and Minorca to the English Crown, the destruction of the defences of Dunkirk, a monopoly of the slave trade for an English company, and the recognition of the Protestant Succession. The other treaties provided for the separation of the Crowns of France and Spain, for the establishment of a Dutch barrier in Belgium, and for the compensation of the Emperor. At the same time a separate peace was negotiated with the Duke of Savoy. Thus French diplomacy, ever resilient, had at last split the coalition asunder. The Austrians and the Dutch were furious at the behaviour of the English Tories, but they had little moral basis for their indignation since both had in the past themselves concluded separate agreements with the French. In spite of their resentment they agreed to send representatives to a peace congress which was to discuss the preliminaries and draw up a definitive treaty. The Congress met at Utrecht in January 1712.

As was the custom at that time, the military campaign continued while the plenipotentiaries haggled, each side hoping that a victory in the field would lend weight to their arguments at the conference table. The Duke of Marlborough was relieved by the Duke of Ormonde, who was given secret orders not to fight a pitched battle while the negotiations were in progress. Prince Eugene, however, returned from Germany and took command of an Anglo-Dutch army based on Douai. The French had lost their last line of fortresses after the previous two campaigns, and could only construct a makeshift line to obstruct the roads leading to the centre of the kingdom. Louis XIV sent for Villars and said: "I have been punished by God; I have richly deserved it, but let us forget our sorrows over domestic fortunes and see what can be done to save the State." He warned the Marshal that he was charged with the command of the last army of France and that if it were beaten the road to Paris would lie open: "I know the Somme," said the King. "It is difficult to cross; there are some points that may be defended: if necessary I shall myself go to Peronne or Saint-Quentin and there collect all the troops I can find, and meet you there. Together we will make a last effort to save our country or perish in the attempt, for I will never allow the enemy to approach my capital." "The most heroic decisions are often the wisest," answered Villars.

Villars conducted operations with profound and unusual caution. In July Eugene took Le Quesnoy and invested Landrecies, the last town covering the route to Paris. The French marshal finally decided to commit his army to the attack, but hesitated between trying to relieve Landrecies and launching a flank attack against Eugene's line of communications. Eventually, after feinting in the direction of Landrecies Villars doubled back during the night of July 23 and delivered an assault upon his enemy's line of communications where they crossed the river Scheldt at Denain. Denain was guarded by eight thousand German and Dutch troops under the Earl of Albemarle. Taken by surprise and overwhelmed by superior numbers, scarcely three thousand of Albemarle's men escaped; many were drowned in the river. The French losses were only four hundred. It was not a big victory but it was decisive. The siege of Landrecies was raised and Le Quesnoy, Douai, and Bouchaim were recaptured. After the victory the Allies, one by one, led by Tory England, whose armies had played no part in the campaign, signed armistices or peace treaties. On April 11, 1713, treaties were concluded at Utrecht between France, on the one hand, and Great Britain, the Dutch Republic, Portugal, Savoy, and Prussia on the other. The preliminary terms secretly agreed to with Great Britain were now confirmed. To the Dutch Louis XIV yielded Belgium, which they were to transfer to the sovereignty of the House of Austria as soon as an understanding had been reached over their "barrier." Louis recognized Anne as Queen of England and the Elector of Brandenburg as King of Prussia. The Electors of Bavaria and of Cologne and Victor Amadeus of Savoy (who also acquired Sicily) were restored to their estates. The King of Portugal received back all his territories. But the crucial clauses of these Treaties were those which affirmed that Louis XIV's grandson was to remain in possession of Spain and the Indies, while the Italian territories of Spain were to pass to the Habsburgs.

The two original claimants to the Spanish heritage still remained to be soothed or satisfied. King Philip V was eventually persuaded by his French advisers to accept the agreed terms, and his renunciation of the French throne and the partition of the Spanish Empire were ratified by the Cortes. The Emperor Charles VI (the former Archduke Charles) was forced by numerous defeats in the field ultimately to acquiesce in the general settlement. After Villars had taken Landau and Freiburg once again, the Treaty of Radstadt was signed between the two commanders (March 16, 1714). By its terms France retained Strasbourg but gave back Landau, Freiburg, and Kehl to the Empire.

Who won the war of the Spanish Succession? On the face of it, after years of perilous and exhausting struggle Louis XIV had achieved the object for which he had gone to war: he had secured universal recognition for his grandson as King of Spain. But the Empire over which Philip of Anjou was to rule had been dismembered.

Louis XIV had in fact gained much less than England and Holland had been willing to concede to him by the Second Partition Treaty of 1700. For the manner in which he had compelled his grandson to accept the partition of the Spanish Empire did much to alienate the governments of France and Spain. Once again history had shown how fallacious is the idea that rulers who belong to the same family bring their countries together (George V of England was the first cousin of Kaiser Wilhelm II). Moreover, the Utrecht settlement brought about that aggrandizement of the House of Austria (by adding to it Belgium and a large part of Italy) which Richelieu and Mazarin had tried to avoid. Equally it strengthened the British Empire while diminishing the chances of French expansion in the New World.

Judged from the longer-term view, as history may judge, the war of the Spanish Succession had created new enemies for France. For while it is true that both Germany and Italy were then still only geographical expressions, Louis XIV's enforced recognition of the Hohenzollern King of Prussia, whose prestige his policy had helped to enhance, and his handing over of Sicily and Nice to the House of Savoy, created two dynasties of which the one proved a serious danger and the other an embarrassment to France in later years. But it is neither just nor reasonable to lay these distant consequences at the door of Louis XIV. The splitting of the Spanish Empire, the expansion of England, the unification of Germany and Italy in the nineteenth century would probably have come about had he never lived. It is easy for historians to erect themselves into moral judges—it is indeed a temptation none can resist—and to persuade themselves that had they been the responsible statesmen whose lives they are describing in full knowledge of the facts, they would have acted far otherwise. But one thing may be ventured, that seldom in the history of modern Europe have nations achieved permanent greatness through deliberately aggressive acts of war, for they invariably overreach themselves. The War of the Spanish Succession, which reduced France to the point of complete exhaustion, of moral and financial bankruptcy, accords with this generalization. But it had proved something different and more important: it had shown in 1709–10, when France had been forced on to the defensive and (in the words of Sir Winston Churchill) "Justice had collected her trappings and crossed to the other camp," that Frenchmen were capable of supreme courage, unity, and self-sacrifice. In those dark days the French spirit proved itself—not for the first nor last time—to be immortal.

An air of emptiness touched with sadness pervaded the last months of the French King's reign. After the death of the attractive and popular Duchess of Burgundy there was little real pleasure left in the Court life of Versailles. Louis found tranquility in the company of a narrowing circle, that of his morganatic wife, his widowed sister-in-law the Duchess of Orleans, his widowed granddaughter by marriage the Duchess of Berri, and his two illegitimate sons. Perhaps he grew more tolerant in his old age; the Duchess of Orleans records that he "let his children and grandchildren take tobacco although they know that it displeases him." Mme de Maintenon protected and cared for him in the intimacies of his private life. When the conversation turned upon the three Dauphins and the Dauphine who had all died, she quickly changed it. But the memory of their unforeseen deaths was never far from the thoughts of the King and his entourage: "We saw the aged were left and that death had swept the young away."

The King's main political activities consisted in clarifying his relations with Spain and in preparing for the Regency that must follow his death. The future Louis XV, "the little Dauphin with very dark big eyes, a chubby face, and a pretty little mouth" which, however, like that of his uncle, was "kept open too much," was only five years old in 1715. The King's plan was to make

certain that the Council of Regency should include all
his most trusted advisers, while his nephew, Philip of
Orleans, who by recognized custom ought to have been
the sole Regent, was only to be the chairman of a
committee of fourteen. Louis succeeded in inducing the
Parliament of Paris to register a decree legitimizing the
Duke of Maine and the Count of Toulouse, thereby
making them the next successors to the Crown if Louis
XV were to die young. In practice it may be doubted
whether either of these princes would have been allowed
to become king. Much to the disgust of the aristocracy
they were also nominated members of the Regency
Council. It is strange that Louis should have imagined
that his wishes as to the future Regency arrangements
would be respected if they were embodied in his will.
Did he not remember across the years that his own father
had tried to dictate the composition of the Regency and
that his orders had been ignored? Louis XIV's own desires were equally to be disregarded.

In Spain, a few months after the death of his first
queen King Philip V married the strong-minded Princess
Elizabeth Farnese. This marriage accentuated the anti-
French tendencies of the Court at Madrid. The Princess
of Ursins, who had become the chief instrument of French
policy at that Court and was deservedly to be rewarded
with a generous pension by Louis XIV, was ignominiously
thrust out of the kingdom into the winter snow, and although the French army was put at the disposal of
Philip V to enable him to deal with his still rebellious
Catalonian subjects, it could be said that the Pyrenees
still existed. In spite of so many years of war Louis did
not even then discard his bellicose outlook, for one of
his last letters concerned a plan to help restore the exiled
Jacobites to the English throne by force of arms.

The King's will was signed in August 1714. From
about that time a decline in his health became notice-
able, although he continued to work as hard as ever.
In the spring of 1715 news of his declining health began

to spread abroad. In August 1715 he left Marly for Versailles to prepare for the end: dark patches on his leg were evidence of gangrene. The calm manner in which he conducted the last affairs of his personal life well accorded with the dignity of royalty. "The King's courage is beyond description," wrote his sister-in-law. "He gives his orders as if he were only going on a journey." He took leave of the great world without regret; his faith in his religion was complete, but in the last months of his life he is said sometimes to have let fall the expression "when I was king." On August 25, the day of St. Louis, he expressed the wish to be serenaded by the fifes and drums of the French and Swiss Guards. He dined that day in public whilst violins and oboes played in his ante-chamber. In the afternoon his confessor, Father Le Tellier (successor of La Chaise), asked him if he was ready to receive Extreme Unction—that Sacrament which he himself had carried to the bed of his grandson, the Duke of Berri, only a year before. On August 30, he had ordered Mme de Maintenon to leave for St. Cyr out of regard for her health and safety. He had already provided for her in the modest way which was all she desired. He thanked his ministers and courtiers with courtesy for their service, commended the Dauphin to the care of the guardians whom he had selected, and recited the "Ave Maria" and the Creed for the last time. He died in the early morning of Sunday, September 1, 1715.

No sooner was the King dead than the courtiers who had been conspiring around his bed set to work. They were well aware that a new age was dawning, though of its real nature they had not the slightest suspicion. The people of Paris, who especially rejoiced at the passing of Louis XIV, may perhaps have had a shrewder idea of the future. But it was indeed a cruel commentary upon this long and, in some respects, glorious reign that it could be recorded that "the common people . . . openly returned thanks to God" when they learned of the death of their King. Posterity may take a more balanced view. Its judgment can be that although Louis XIV may not himself have earned all the commendations lavished upon him by his contemporaries, yet the magnificent progress achieved during his reign in the arts, in the sciences, and in the industrial life of his country yield him at least a reflected glory; his reign crystallized and he himself symbolized the greatness of his nation.

Chapter 12

The Greatness of France

HISTORY HAS ON THE WHOLE been severe on Louis XIV. The critics gathered round his death-bed. The Duke of Saint-Simon, that class-conscious aristocrat, whose attractive and voluminous memoirs provide so much information for all writers on this period, after sourly commenting upon the King's many errors of judgment, said that his passing was regretted by none but his valets and a few old courtiers. The German Ezechiel Spanheim's contemporary opinion was that the King "had loved glory too much at the expense of his real greatness." Another contemporary assigned this spurious phrase to the dying King: "I have been too fond of war."

The King's autocracy, his extravagance, his delight in flattery, the relative failure of his aggressive foreign policy, the evil consequences of his religious policy, his inability to cope with the economic problems of his subjects, are all on detailed record for study and disapprobation. It is perhaps easy to forget the triumphs of the early part of the reign in the disasters of which men like Saint-Simon and Spanheim wrote. But in any case the new Europe, which dawned with the French Revolution, and which dissolved into the middle-class era of Louis Philippe and Queen Victoria, was scarcely likely to be appreciative of the "Sun King." French republican ardour, anti-clerical indignation, or English puritan morality has flavoured the approach of many of the writers on Louis XIV. His champions have been romantics or sycophants like Voltaire. Even the most knowledgeable and impartial historians have been censorious. Michelet spoke of the "financial and moral bankruptcy" of the end of the reign. Ernest Lavisse wrote that Louis had "exhausted" his kingdom. MM. de Saint

Léger and Sagnac have recently written: "Louis XIV, without any preconceived plan, had gradually formed a grand design which he tried to realize during his reign, and which he never abandoned (except in part owing to force): the absolute submission of his subjects to his orders and the complete submission of Europe"; both plans failed.

Lord Acton described Louis XIV as by far the ablest man born in modern times on the steps of a throne. Although one may not be able to go as far as this, it is perhaps the fairest way to judge him. Louis cannot be blamed because he was not a nineteenth-century constitutional reformer. At least he regarded his profession and his religion seriously. At least when he decided a point of policy he took all the available advice and considered the question from every angle before he finally made up his mind. Sainte-Beuve says that his only natural gift was common sense and plenty of it. Most men with his upbringing and in his position would probably have reached much the same decisions.

All historians would at any rate agree that Louis XIV was a superlatively conscientious king. His application and his interest in every subject that came within his orbit emerge clearly from the rather turgid verbiage of his so-called *Memoirs*. In these *Memoirs* there is none of the bold sweep or daring generalization about the art of government that is to be found, say, in the writings of Napoleon. Louis's theme is that every royal action is closely followed and criticized; people may make a mockery of a King's mistakes, but since he is supreme there is no one whom he himself can blame. Consequently Louis was of the opinion that a monarch must try to familiarize himself with a wide range of subjects so as not to depend unduly upon his advisers and so as to be able to handle in particular any questions of policy that might be raised by foreign ambassadors. This intense degree of application has its weaknesses. For the ideal executive is the man who keeps a clear desk and sends for his subordinates when he requires a set of facts or figures. The absence from Louis XIV's literary remains of any valuable reflections on the art of government may well be explained by the fact that he too often allowed himself to be absorbed in a mass of detail.

The second important consequence of the King's profound devotion to duty was that after his early years he never permitted himself to relax or unbend. This is hard on his biographers, but is characteristic of many public figures. It is true that Thackeray produced a famous cartoon of Louis XIV in which he contrasted the monarch fully arrayed in his robes and wig with the bald pot-bellied male underneath. But few of us look dignified when we are undressed. And the significant point about Louis XIV is that he was very careful that he never *did* undress in public. He was always serious, affable, ceremonious, cautious—and always the master. Every event in the royal life had to be considered and planned with the utmost gravity. It would have ill become a godlike ruler to be touched by the ordinary emotions of common humanity. Versailles knew wit but little honest laughter.

Some writers indeed, thinking largely in terms of the second half of the reign, have reflected upon the joylessness of the age as a whole; they dilate upon the cynicism of the epigrams of La Rochefoucauld, they recall that Molière died of melancholia, they emphasize that the King had no sense of humour. All this shows a lack of proportion. For France was not the Court, that narrow circle of rich idlers who would have liked to ignore the rest of the world if they could. The true France was represented by the soldiers who manned the entrenchments at Malplaquet, the sailors who punished the Mediterranean pirates and conquered the great de Ruyter, the savants who sailed to Siam happily discussing philosophy, the prosperous bourgeoisie depicted by Molière, the hard-working administrators and diplomatists, the peasants and craftsmen who made French decorative arts and food and wine famous throughout the civilized world. The greatness of France lay in men and things like these, and the Court of Versailles was merely the passing symbol of their glory.

In trying to put the reign of Louis XIV into historical perspective it is a mistake to attribute to one man the direction of historical movements which led to the French Revolution. His immediate successor, the Regent Orleans, reversed his policy in many respects, but found himself equally subject to that inertia in institutions and selfishness in men which together dam, or try to dam, the flow of events and so sooner or later produce catastrophe.

Louis XIV may perhaps most easily be condemned for his foreign policy. Criticism is well summarized by Charles Seignobos in these terms: "Louis XIV fortified by his policy of magnificence the incomparable position won for France by the policy of the Cardinals." At the beginning of the reign the French Government was able to dominate Europe; the majority of the German princes were its allies—so too were the rulers of England and Holland. But Louis dissipated his resources upon foolish minor quarrels and created an atmosphere of distrust before he began to seek territorial expansion. Although it is clear from his *Memoirs* that he understood the importance of extending the frontiers of France to the north-east and to the line of the Rhine, he came to jeopardize his opportunities by pursuing the mirage of the Spanish Succession. By his conduct he threw away the goodwill built up by his diplomatists and wasted the victories won by his soldiers.

Territorial aggrandizement is not in itself a commendable object of policy; but the search for security is at least understandable. A policy of mere prestige can have little justification. And what Louis XIV did was to sacrifice security to prestige. This was fully proved when in 1701 he took the decision to accept the will of Charles II of Spain rather than abide by the Partition Treaty. For the Treaty would have given France supremacy in the Mediterranean and the chance for an African empire for which she was to scramble in the nineteenth

century, whereas all that the will offered France was a
personal triumph for his own family. At tremendous, indeed almost irreparable, cost to his country, he succeeded in placing his grandson upon the throne of Spain.
But the unwisdom of this policy was shown when in
1718, three years after his death, the French Government entered into a Quadruple Alliance against Spain
and sent an army against Madrid. As Voltaire wrote,
"the first war of Louis XV was against his uncle whom
Louis XIV had established at such cost." On the other
hand, France had to wait twenty years to exact by the
Treaty of Vienna the reversion of Lorraine which Louis
XIV could have acquired without war but had refused
—a more valuable acquisition than any of his conquests.

In matters of internal administration Louis XIV had
inherited the policy of centralization. The conduct of
the nobles and of the provinces during his minority
when they plunged the country into civil war left him
with no alternative but to insist upon an absolutist régime
and to seek his ministers among the middle classes. But
a highly centralized absolutist government depends upon
the life of one individual; and when that individual is a
hereditary monarch, the chances of the system breaking
down are considerable. Neither Louis XV nor Louis
XVI measured up to Louis XIV's own modest but hard-
working standards. It was said of Louis XV that he would
"only give an hour a day to business." Louis XVI was
tired out by any intellectual labour and fell asleep in the
council chamber. The policy of prestige, the diffusion
of royal solemnity, and, in the later stages of the reign,
the example of devotion, were the necessary professional
equipment of a godlike King. Louis XIV's successors
were not godlike. The Regent lived a life of dissipation
which smothered the best intentions. Louis XV detested
etiquette and everything that Versailles represented.
Hereditary absolutism is a system that can never work.
Louis XIV recognized as much himself when he tried to
place his illegitimate sons in the line of succession and
thrust them into the Council of Regency. The only way

in which such a method of government can perpetuate
itself is by allowing strong ministers—Mayors of the
Palace, Grand Vizirs, or Shoguns—to take over the real
direction of affairs as soon as a weakling inherits the
throne. Alternatively absolutism must modify itself by
offering concessions to the most influential classes. Louis
XIV made one such concession by choosing his ministers
from the middle classes, but he would not give them a
free hand and never admitted their indispensability. His
refusal to summon the States-General for consultation at
the crisis of his reign was logical. But it lay in the logic
of history (and in its irony too) that a centralized administration, a States-General which refused to dissolve,
and middle-class ministers with radical ideas were to be
three of the main features of the French Revolution.

If the distant pattern of the Revolution may be detected in the reign of Louis XIV, so too the social causes
of the Revolution may be found there. Whatever were
the ultimate forces which brought the Revolution about,
all historians agree that one of the biggest grievances to
attract discontent in the eighteenth century was the contrast between the privileges of the nobility and clergy and
the burdens of the peasantry. It was Louis XIV who
fashioned that unjustifiable social institution, the Court
nobility—four thousand families who shared 33,000,000
livres of pensions between them and owned 4,000,000,-
000 livres' worth of property and spent their incomes like
water on fêtes, hunting parties, and receptions but were
allowed no duties and devoted their energies to intrigue
or conspiracy. The provincial nobility, worse off finan-
cially, were equally without functions. They irritated their
tenants by exacting from them hunting rights, tithes, and
tolls and enforcing their claims by judicial means. Their
mode of living was a burden both to the peasantry and
to themselves. As economic conditions began to improve
in the eighteenth century the French peasants grew even
more conscious of the social inequalities under which
they strained—grievances which had become all the more
conspicuous in the reign of Louis XIV.

The general misery of the ordinary people of France at the time of Louis XIV's death is well attested. The primary cause was fiscal. The heavy cost of the long and unsuccessful wars which had begun in 1688 and 1701 and, to a lesser extent, royal extravagance, had increased the pressure of taxation and demanded the invention of dubious financial expedients. The main tax, the taille, fell almost entirely upon agriculture and upon the poorer classes. Peasants frequently had their cattle seized for failing to pay. Many farmers voluntarily abandoned their land because they were unable to meet their obligations. In 1697, when a short interval of peace was beginning, the Intendants (the provincial governors of France) were instructed to carry out a detailed enquiry into the conditions throughout the countryside. Their memorials (though incomplete) all agreed that the incidence of taxation and the arbitrary nature of the fiscal system were the chief grievances of the people at large. No minister had the courage to try to remedy this state of affairs. All kinds of devices were tried—such as the introduction of lotteries and the depreciation of the currency—but these only made the situation far worse. By 1715 the Government was in debt to the extent of some 3,000,000,000 livres— a colossal sum for those days.

The bankruptcy of the French Government was a fair reflection of the general condition of the national economy. The Intendants' memorials of 1697 indeed bore fresh witness that the situation of the countryside was desperate, and there was still to come the long and exhausting war of the Spanish Succession, which brought widespread famine in its train. Wars were equally damaging to French commerce, for the European countries which combined to defeat Louis XIV's armies ceased in a large measure to be the customers of France, while they had been already discouraged from exchanging goods with the French by Colbert's rigid Protectionism. By the end of the seventeenth century the activity of the western ports of France was beginning to decline and they were losing their business to the ports of Spain and Portugal. In spite of this fall in foreign trade, however, French industry was not hit as severely as agriculture by the conditions of the last years of the reign. French agriculture, however, had seldom been less prosperous.

France took a long time to recover from the effects of the reign. It is a mistake to imagine that the lot of the French peasant in the eighteenth century steadily improved (as De Tocqueville argued) in spite of the impositions of an outworn system of national and local taxation. French agriculture made little real progress between the accession of Louis XIV and the Revolution; fiscal burdens and inheritance laws often drove peasant proprietors into becoming labourers or mortagaging their produce to meet their obligations. Industry, on the other hand, prospered —partly under the impulse given it by the paternalism of Colbert—and a working class in the modern sense came into existence. It was this combination of a new industrial class, a discontented peasantry, and an active middle class prepared to undertake political leadership which makes the French Revolution a turning-point in the history of modern Europe. Nearly all the factors which prepared the way may be seen in the reign of Louis XIV.

Religion is a pillar of monarchy, and a simple elemental faith is always looked for by those who fashion the aggressive nation State. In modern Japan Shintoism overrode both Buddhism and Christianity: the German National-Socialists tried to invent a "German Christianity." So, in Louis XIV's France, his Ministers of State took drastic measures to fit all forms of the Christian religion into a single Gallican pattern. Not only was French Protestantism suppressed by methods of extraordinary rigour and vileness but all unorthodox forms of Catholicism, from Jansenism to the harmless contemplative faith of the Quietists, were attacked at the direct behest of the monarchy. Bossuet dictated the faith of his countrymen with a majestic and persuasive eloquence that recalled St. Bernard of Clairvaux; but he did not live in the Middle Ages. Already the voice of "reason" and the claim of "natural laws" were beginning to be heard; and it has often been pointed out that not only were there gentle hints of scepticism in the writings of great Frenchmen like Molière and La Fontaine, but the philosophy of Descartes and later the ponderous learning of Bayle's encyclopedia were starting to undermine the structure of orthodoxy before Louis XIV died. But what was more important was that the quarrels among Christians, the undignified tussles between the French King and the Pope, and the punishments to which single-hearted men and women of harmless faiths were subjected helped to create anti-clericalism and by discrediting the French Church discredited Christianity itself. Voltaire and the French Encyclopedists of the eighteenth century preached to a receptive audience because the leaders of French Christianity had engaged in internecine warfare a half-century earlier. The Jesuit Order was suppressed in France in 1762 partly at least because the Jesuits had abused their positions of authority when they had the ear of the King.

The questioning spirit which made itself felt by way of reaction to the rigid orthodoxy of Louis XIV was not limited to matters of religion. In his remarkable book *Télémaque* written during the latter part of the reign for the benefit of Louis's heir apparent, the Duke of Burgundy, Archbishop Fénelon had attacked the very bases of political autocracy, while Vauban, in his book that was suppressed, severely criticized the principles of economic privilege on which the old régime rested. But in the history of modern Europe it is seldom that ideas battle with ideas upon equal terms. The test of political practices is invariably pragmatical. The last years of Louis XIV's reign saw the seeds of revolutionary ideas being sown not because people were logically persuaded that the institutions of absolute monarchy were wrong in themselves but because they had ceased to give material satisfaction to any but a small minority of French society. As Lord Morley wrote, "A dignified and venerable hierarchy, an august and powerful monarchy, a court of gay and luxurious nobles, all lost their grace, because the eyes of men were suddenly caught and appalled by the awful phantom, which was yet so real, of a perishing nation." The legacy of Louis XIV, admitted Lytton Strachey, himself the unstinted admirer of the Augustan age of Louis XIV, was poverty, discontent, tyranny, and fanaticism.

How astounding was this contrast between the misery of the common people and the glories of Versailles over which the King presided for so many years! Did he not know when he sacrificed everything to put his grandson upon the throne of Spain the price he was making his people pay? Without an appreciation of this contrast in the late seventeenth and early eighteenth centuries one cannot understand the real nature of the background against which Rousseau preached the equality of man and Voltaire questioned the consolations of official religion. And yet the reign of Louis XIV was looked upon by contemporaries as an age of stability, an age of classical dignity, of strong Catholic faith, and of autocratic solidarity. Contemporary England had passed through a series of revolutions and had beheaded one king and dethroned another. It had also witnessed the birth of nonconformity and the spread of scepticism. But eighteenth-century France was in a constant turmoil, whilst eighteenth-century England at any rate until the Industrial Revolution was reckoned a peaceful and quiet land, with few problems to solve, unhurried and unromantic. Though Montesquieu and Voltaire were to bring back a budgetful of ideas from their visits to England, the dynamic character of French history in the eighteenth century was the direct consequence not of foreign influence so much as the inability of Louis XIV to deal drastically with the pressing problems of the mass of his subjects. Perhaps it is true, however, as Lord Acton wrote, that France needed this interval of Louis XIV's reign with all its superficial splendour and measured dignity before moving forward into the modern world of industrialism and democracy.

To the foreign student of France the reflection that always recurs in reading her history is how the spirit and genius of her people invariably overcome the errors of her rulers. M. Sagnac wrote that in spite of Louis XIV's failure to put his heritage to good use, so that his reign ended in general misery and discontent, the vitality of the French spirit made individual progress possible. In the reigns both of Louis XIV and of Louis XV the literature and art of France, mirroring the movements and outlook of the changing times, were always virile and influential. What other country in the world would have been capable of producing great poetry, prose, and pictorial art, as France did, during the soul-destroying years of the German National-Socialist occupation? The rulers of France may change, be unworthy or tyrannical, but her native genius endures undiminished.

At different phases in the history of modern France her citizens have found inspiration in looking backwards towards the reign of Louis XIV and reminding themselves of the political leadership which their country then enjoyed in Europe. Louis Bertrand prefaces his entertaining book on Louis XIV, written after the war of 1914–1918, by describing how he had gazed upon the equestrian statue of Louis XIV at Montpelier and meditated upon the greatness of his country; Lord Acton, lecturing to his Cambridge students some thirty years earlier, told them that Louis XIV gave the French people the feeling of unity which they needed after generations of civil wars. All who today stroll in peace through the gardens of Versailles may share too in the consciousness of the continuing glory of France which Louis XIV once represented.

For Further Reading

The reign of Louis XIV was prolific in first-rate memoir and letter writers, many of whom have been translated into English. The most useful and entertaining are perhaps:

MME DE LA FAYETTE:
   Mémoires de la Cour de France (Petitot collection II, 64, 65. 1819).
LOUIS XIV:
   Mémoires (ed. Jean Longnon, 1928).
MME DE MOTTEVILLE:
   Memoirs of Anne of Austria and her Court (abridged translation, 3 vols., ed. K. P. Wormeley. 1902).
ELIZABETH CHARLOTTE, DUCHESS OF ORLEANS:
   Secret Memoirs (English abridgment of correspondence. 1895).
L. DE SAINT-SIMON:
   Mémoires (ed. Boislisle). (English abridgment by K. P. Wormeley, 4 vols.)
   Parallèle des Trois Rois (ed. Faugère. 1880).

(For an interesting evaluation of Saint-Simon as an historian, see M. Langlois, *Saint-Simon comme historien,* Revue Historique, 158.)

MME DE SÉVIGNÉ:
   Letters (English abridgment, 2 vols. 1927).
L. H. DE VILLARS:
   Mémoires (ed. Vogüé. 1884–1904).
J. B. P. VISCONTI:
   Mémoires de la Cour de Louis XIV (ed. Lemoine. 1908).

The best among a rather mixed collection of secondary authorities are probably:

A. BARINE:
   Louis XIV et la Grande Mademoiselle (1905).
M. A. GEFFROY:
   Mme de Maintenon d'après sa correspondance authentique (1887).
A. HASSALL:
   Louis XIV (1895).

E. LAVISSE:
  Histoire de France, vol. 7, i–ii, 1643–1685; vol. 8, i, 1685–1715 (1902).

G. LACOUR-GAYET:
  L'Education politique de Louis XIV (1898).

E. LODGE:
  Sully, Colbert, Turgot (1931).

G. MARTIN:
  Histoire de la Nation Française, vol. X: *Economique et Financière* (1927).
  La Grande Industrie sous Louis XIV (1899).

P. DE NOLHAC:
  La Création de Versailles (1925).

C. G. PICAVET:
  La Diplomatie Française au Temps de Louis XIV (1930).

C. B. DE LA RONCIÈRE:
  Histoire de la Marine Française,, vols. V and VI (1920, 1932).

C. SEIGNOBOS:
  A History of the French People (English trans. 1933).

G. LYTTON STRACHEY:
  Landmarks in French Literature (1923).

A. DE VOLTAIRE:
  Le Siècle de Louis XIV (Librairie Garnier).

Since the first impression of this book was published the following have become available:

LOUIS ANDRÉ:
  Louis XIV et L'Europe (1950), (an apologia with bibliography).

JAMES E. KING:
  Science and Rationalism in the Government of Louis XIV (1949) (ingenious but not convincing).

A. DE SAINT LÉGER AND PHILIPPE SAGNAC:
  La Prépondérance Française sous Louis XIV, 1661–1715 (1949) (admirable and well balanced).

Popular books recently published in English are H. CARRÉ: *The Early Life of Louis XIV* (1951); W. H. LEWIS: *The Splendid Century* (1953); W. H. LEWIS: *Louis XIV* (1959); and M. SUTHERLAND: *Louis XIV and Marie Mancini* (1956). I should also mention the little book on Louis XIV by my old teacher, Mr. David Ogg, published in 1933.

Index

190 / Index